LOVE YOUR NAYBA

30 stories of
churches transforming
neighbourhoods

PublishU Ltd

www.PublishU.com

Acknowledgments

Creative Director:

Matt Bird

Design, Copywriting and Research:

Nurden Cross

Cover Image:

Johnny Miller

www.unequalscenes.com

Used With Permission

Other Images supplied
by the Projects
or sourced from
Unsplash and Pexels

Thanks to God for his love
and the tangible love of his Church
around the world.

CONTENTS

FOREWORD

Countries, Monarchs and Governments may change but the work of the global church in communities around the world remains.

When Jesus was asked what really mattered in life he responded, to love God and "love your nayba" (Belize Kriol Bible, Matthew 19:19) which is why our global foundation is called NAYBA and we help churches love their neighbours and transform their neighbourhoods.

There are times when we all experience vulnerability, isolation and loneliness and it is during these times in our lives that we particularly need our neighbours to provide tangible love and practical help.

This coffee table book tells the stories of some of the human pain and need in our world today but also the beautiful, generous and kind ways the global church is loving their neighbours in a way that transforms neighbourhoods.

I hope you are as inspired to read this as it was for us to write it!

Matt Bird
Founder CEO
NAYBA
mattbird@nayba.org

This amazing collection of Love Your NAYBA stories is an incredible testimony to the invitation of Christ to "Love one another" (John 13:34).

It speaks to two other messages of Jesus that we must recognise in celebration of this work.

Firstly, each of these NAYBA stories represents a practical application of the message of Jesus who said, “I came that they may have life, and have it abundantly!” (John 10:10).

Secondly, as a project this book represents the light that Jesus calls on his followers to become: “You are the light of the world!” (Matthew 5:14). It challenges us to do what is within our capacity to do, to light up against the dark gloom of the hardship of life for our NAYBA.

In the isiXhosa language of South Africa we say “Isandla sihlamba esinye” - the hand washes the other. In the words of Jesus this book says, “Go and do likewise” (Luke 10:37).

Rt Rev Malusi Mpumlwana
General Secretary
South African Council of Churches

COMMUNITY PROJECTS

1	**LYRICS AND LUNCH**	United Kingdom	Dementia
2	**MAINLY MINISTRIES**	Australia	Isolated Mothers
3	**VICTORY LANGUAGE SCHOOL**	Albania	Youth Development
4	**THE BEEHIVE**	United Kingdom	Loneliness
5	**EMPOWERED FAITH COMMUNITIES**	Australia	Doing Life Tough
6	**SIKUNYE**	South Africa	Vulnerable Children
7	**UP CAFE**	Albania	Vulnerable Youth
8	**ADOPT-A-POLICE STATION**	South Africa	Crime
9	**CARE FOR EX-OFFENDERS**	Australia	Crime
10	**BOYS TO MEN**	South Africa	Fatherlessness

MATERIAL PROJECTS

WELLBEING PROJECTS

17	**PEACED TOGETHER**	Europe	Broken Women
18	**PROJECT EXODUS**	South Africa	Addiction
19	**CIRCUIT BREAKER**	Australia	Domestic Violence
20	**STEPS COURSE**	Denmark	Low Self-esteem
21	**COACH MENTORING**	Australia	Family Breakdown
22	**EDIFY**	South Africa	Mental Health
23	**SANCTUARY COURSE**	Australia	Anxiety & Depression
24	**LISTENING HUBS**	United Kingdom	Social Isolation
25	**KIDS HOPE**	Australia	Vulnerable Children

ENTERPRISE PROJECTS

COMMUNITY

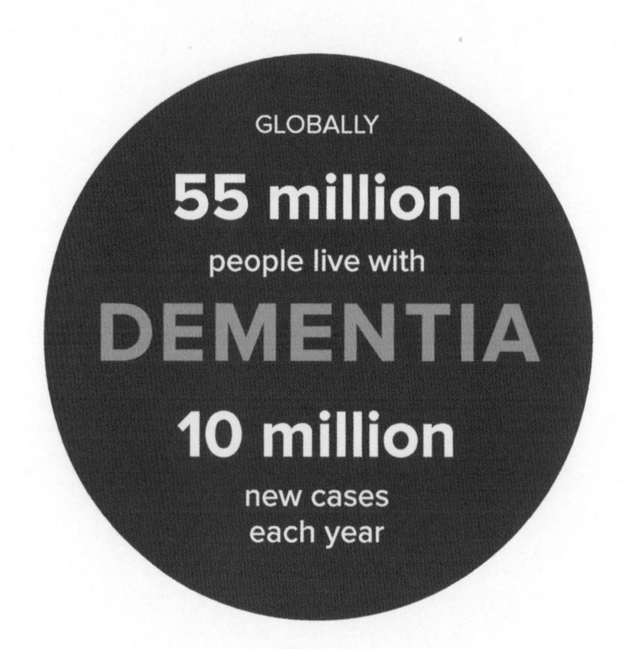
GLOBALLY
55 million
people live with
DEMENTIA
10 million
new cases
each year

LYRICS AND LUNCH

> “
> *It’s the first place I’ve taken him to since his diagnosis, where we can both join in together and he doesn’t stick out like a sore thumb.*
>
> A CARER

LYRICS AND LUNCH

THE NEED

- One of the main challenges for people living with dementia and for their carers, is loneliness.
- Currently more than 55 million people live with dementia worldwide, and there are nearly 10 million new cases every year. [1]
- Dementia has physical, psychological, social and economic impacts, not only for people living with dementia, but also for their carers, families and society at large.
- Music therapy improves the quality of life of people with dementia.

THE PROJECT

Lyrics and Lunch helps the local church to provide friendship and fun for those living with dementia. It comprises a network of friendly singing and lunch groups which creates community for those living with dementia and their carers.

Music is a fantastic way of reaching people with dementia. The brain remembers songs, even the lyrics of songs sung years ago, and it can help them feel normal again for a while.

This programme supports Carers in a really helpful way — giving them lots of chance to share ideas, problems and solutions. Music to feed the brain and lunch to enjoy together!

INGREDIENTS

- Minimum of 6 volunteers who have a compassion for older people
- An attractive space with comfortable seating for the sing-a-long part
- A space to sit at tables close to a kitchen
- A catering plan for producing the food
- Somebody who can lead the singing

METHOD

1. Partner with a church or two in the neighbourhood
2. Recruit 6 volunteers to fulfil specific functions
3. Choose a venue considering facilities and accessibility in the neighbourhood
4. Team Training — participate in the online training provided by Lyrics & Lunch
5. Acquire the Songbook from Lyrics & Lunch

LIVES TRANSFORMED

"I'm 84 years of age and I've been coming to lyrics and lunch now for about five years. My wife was always a singer and when we came to lyrics and lunch, a smile used to come on her face and she so really enjoyed what was taking place. She felt comfortable because there were other people with this same sort of illness as her. I get so much out of coming to Lyrics and Lunch because of the friendliness of the people and also because I can share the difficulties and problems that I experience."

a HUSBAND and CARER

FIND OUT MORE

 *nayba.org/resources/lyrics-and-lunch*

 *@lyricsandlunch*

GLOBALLY

15%

new mothers experience

POST NATAL DEPRESSION

yet 50% cases are
not reported
due to social stigma

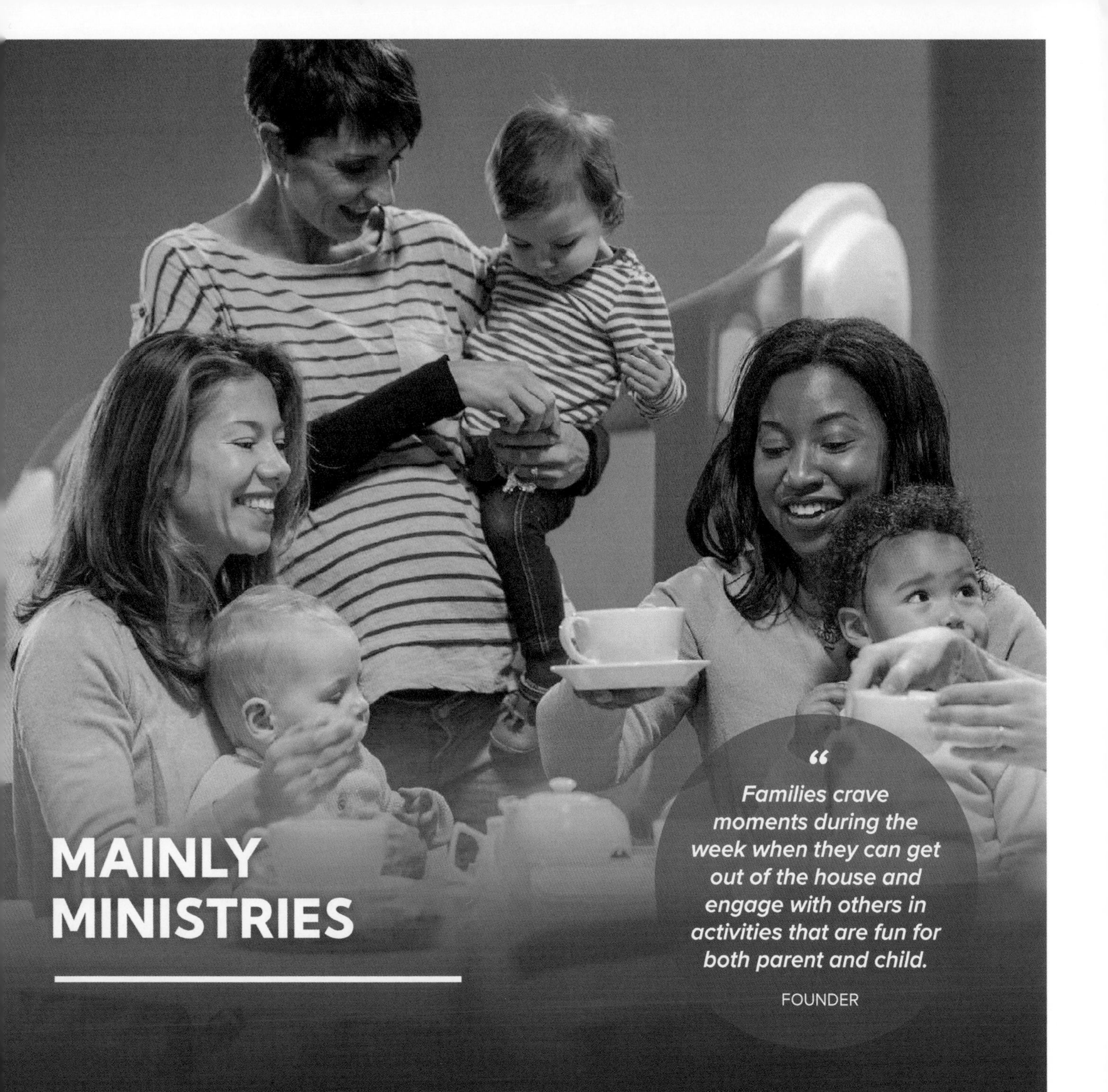

MAINLY MINISTRIES

> *"Families crave moments during the week when they can get out of the house and engage with others in activities that are fun for both parent and child.*
>
> FOUNDER

MAINLY MINISTRIES

THE NEED

- Post natal depression is a mood disorder that affects approximately 10–15% of adult mothers yearly. [2]
- Social connections are imperative for those caring for young children. A 2018 Social Survey in New Zealand indicated half of those parenting on their own experience a level of loneliness some of the time. [2]
- Fear, especially for single parents, fearing how you will parent on your own, is very real. Finding a place of community, where there is no judgement, is an antidote to this anxiety.

THE PROJECT

Mainly Ministries provides solutions that help the local church connect with community families who have young children, by providing a place of belonging, engagement, care and learning. A place where families love to be known and volunteers love to serve.

The programme includes a music session for babies and toddlers and a session designed around the reading of a book. Both are followed by a time of eat/play/chat when refreshments are provided for all. Children then play in an unstructured environment and the adults get to chat.

INGREDIENTS

- A clear purpose – why do you want to connect with local families?
- A perceived need in the community
- A supportive church leadership who understand the value of this programme
- A group of volunteers – eager to be trained
- Suitable place and equipment to meet

METHOD

1. Complete an an application on the **mainlyMinistries** website
2. Receive the set-up pack
3. Train the volunteers through the online resources provided
4. Obtain sign off by a Coach to 'go public'
5. Set up the meeting space
6. Continue receiving resources from **mainly Ministries**

HELPING CHURCHES CONNECT WITH **FAMILIES** WITH **YOUNG CHILDREN** PROVIDING A PLACE OF **CARE** AND **ENGAGEMENT**

LIVES TRANSFORMED

"When your child has a brain tumour at eight months of age, knowing a whole church is praying brings comfort. When your baby then goes through chemotherapy and loses the ability to see, attending any social gathering becomes a sensory overload. But as a parent, you know the value of community and social experience. When the volunteers go to every possible length to be inclusive, to the point of one of them learning braille, your gratefulness is in overload."

a MOTHER

FIND OUT MORE

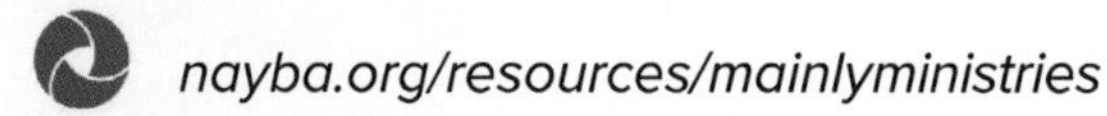
nayba.org/resources/mainlyministries

@mainlymusicmainlyplay

@mainlymusicmainlyplay

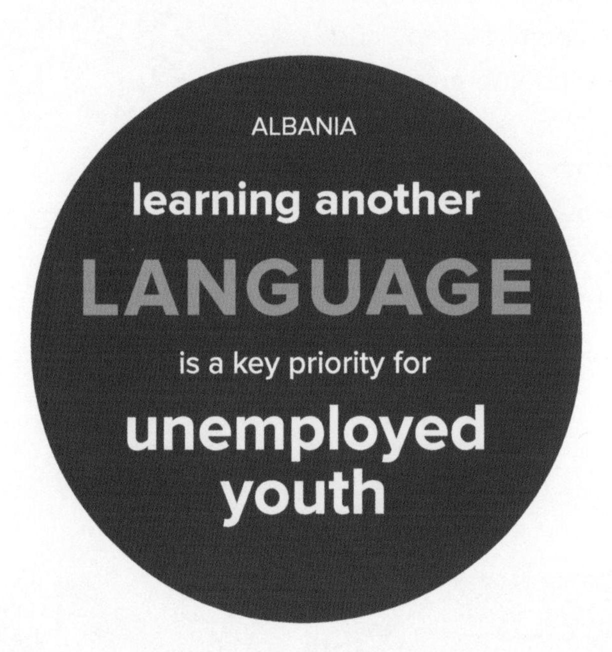
ALBANIA
learning another
LANGUAGE
is a key priority for
unemployed
youth

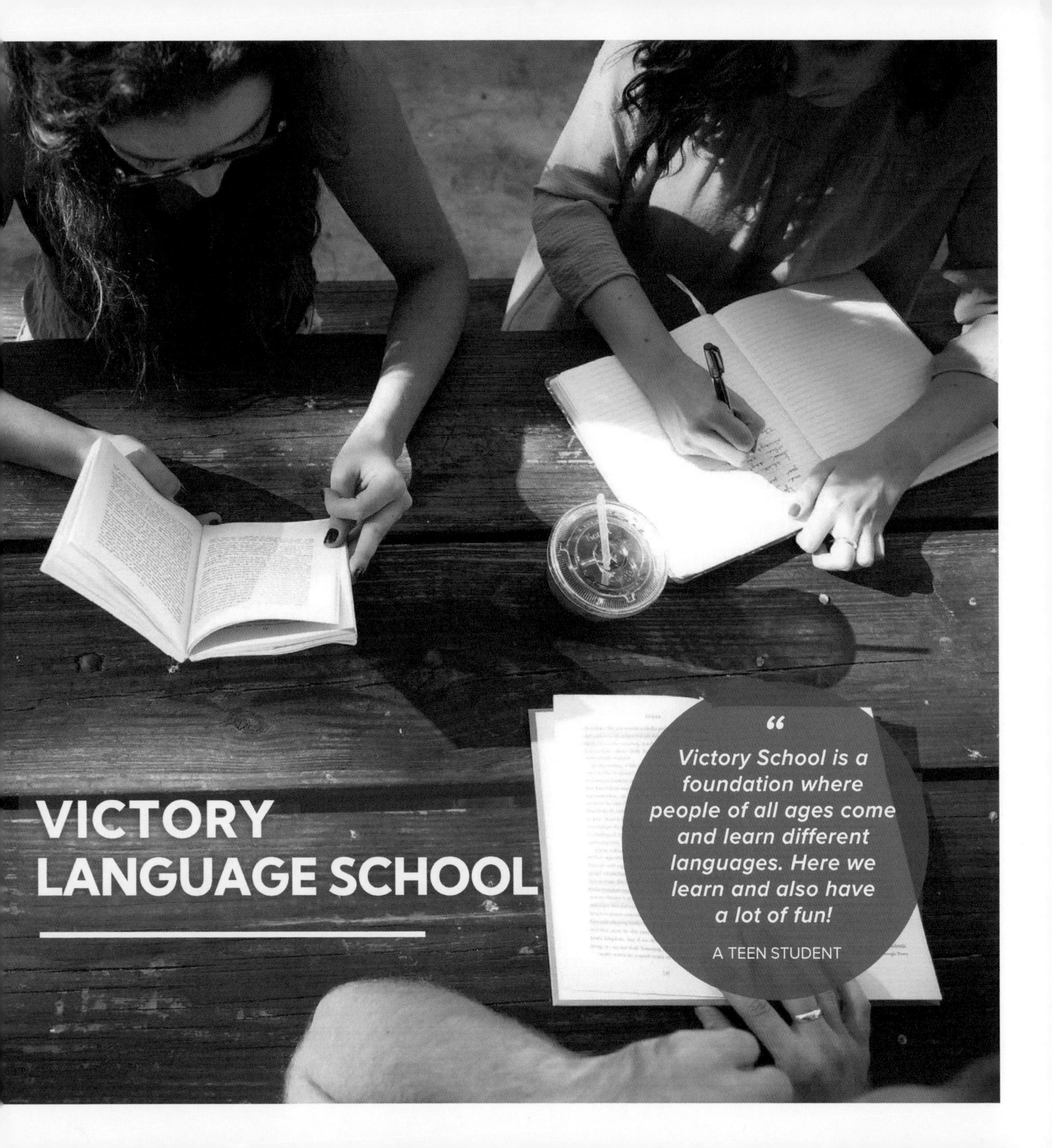
VICTORY
LANGUAGE SCHOOL
"Victory School is a foundation where people of all ages come and learn different languages. Here we learn and also have a lot of fun!
A TEEN STUDENT

VICTORY LANGUAGE SCHOOL

THE NEED

- As Albania emerges from a post communist world, many younger people recognise that one of the key ways to advance economically is to learn one or more languages of Europe.
- The main foreign language spoken in Albania is English at 40 %, followed by Italian at 27.8% and Greek at 22.9%. [3]
- According to a 2014 survey 80% of Albanian youth want to emigrate driven in large part by their concerns about high unemployment (estimated at 29.2%) and poverty, and in pursuit of a better education abroad. [3]

THE PROJECT

The Victory School helps local churches in Albania to teach people of all ages to learn a new language. The school has had a huge impact in the local community where the participants have come from all economic levels and age groups to learn languages that will help them integrate into Europe and improve their future prospects and personal lives.

By providing a space and infrastructure for learning a foreign language, the local church is seen as providing a vital service to the community, and young people are attracted to joining the church as a result.

INGREDIENTS

- A community needing to learn other languages
- A lead volunteer who knows other languages
- Volunteer teachers of foreign languages
- An equipped meeting space suitable as a classroom
- Necessary language learning resources
- Pastoral support for the volunteers and for the participants of the course

METHOD

1. Recruit a lead volunteer and team (min. of 2)
2. Undertake language school training
3. Secure the use of a meeting space, including suitable tables and chairs
4. Obtain literature, apps and weblink to resource the process
5. Recruit course participants through relationships and referrals

HELPING CHURCHES IN **ALBANIA** TO TEACH PEOPLE OF ALL AGE**S TO LEARN A NEW LANGUAGE**

LIVES TRANSFORMED

“When I came here for the first time I had no idea what I was going to do and I was really scared, but having a great teacher and some amazing friends, I found I can do everything I needed to with their support.

It's my third year here and I have passed very well and my English has improved a lot. I'm very proud and glad that I'm student of this school. It has opened a window for our future and we must now learn how to use it in our favour.”

a TEEN STUDENT

FIND OUT MORE

 *nayba.org/resources/victory-school*

 *@victoryschoolalbania*

 *@victoryschool.al*

ENGLAND

45%

of adults experience

LONELINESS

which equates to

25 million

men and women

THE BEEHIVE

> "This is my favourite place! I have been through a rough time and The Beehive is my sanctuary! Always greeted with a smile and a welcome!
>
> EVA

THE BEEHIVE

THE NEED

- 45% of adults feel occasionally, sometimes or often lonely in England. This equates to twenty five million people. [4]
- According to the UK Office for National Statistics, women reported feeling lonely more frequently than men. They were significantly more likely than men to report feeling lonely "often/ always", "some of the time" and "occasionally" and were less likely than men to say they "never" felt lonely.
- Loneliness, living alone and poor social connections are reportedly as bad for your health as smoking 15 cigarettes a day or living with obesity. [4]

THE PROJECT

The Beehive helps the local church to have a visible neutral presence in the heart of the community and offer a social service to the neighbourhood that is both appealing and intriguing. The Beehive is part community coffee shop, part women's clothing boutique and part workshop space with a heart to empower women, helping them to connect with other women and feel beautiful, valued and loved.

The Beehive is a secondhand women's clothing boutique and cafe in the heart of Ashford town centre that aims to make all of its customers feel valued, loved and beautiful. It also serves as a safe space for non-church people to visit and be listened to and even prayed for.

INGREDIENTS

- A lead volunteer who is inspired with team leading and work experience in retail
- A suitable venue that is attractive and highly visible to the local community
- A team of 5 volunteers with various relevant skills and a heart for helping people
- A decent coffee machine
- A supply of donated high quality "pre-loved" clothing

METHOD

1. Launch with a pop-up store over a weekend to test the idea in the community
2. Make an appeal in the church and community for high quality clothing donations
3. Assemble a team of suitable volunteers
4. Find a neutral venue away from the church and highly visible in the community
5. After the launch, evaluate the feasibility of a long-term venture in the local high street

HELPING CHURCHES HAVE A VISIBLE NEUTRAL **PRESENCE IN THE COMMUNITY** AND OFFER **AN APPEALING SERVICE**

LIVES TRANSFORMED

"Literally my favourite place to go in Ashford! I've been through a really hard few months and The Beehive has made it so much easier! From the amazing staff and volunteers to the amazing clothes. I know I can always come in and have a lovely coffee, cake and a good chat which is much needed! Honestly I can't thank The Beehive enough for what they do. You've changed my life and I will always be so grateful!"

LUCY

FIND OUT MORE

 *nayba.org/resources/thebeehive*

 *@beehiveashford*

 *@beehiveashford*

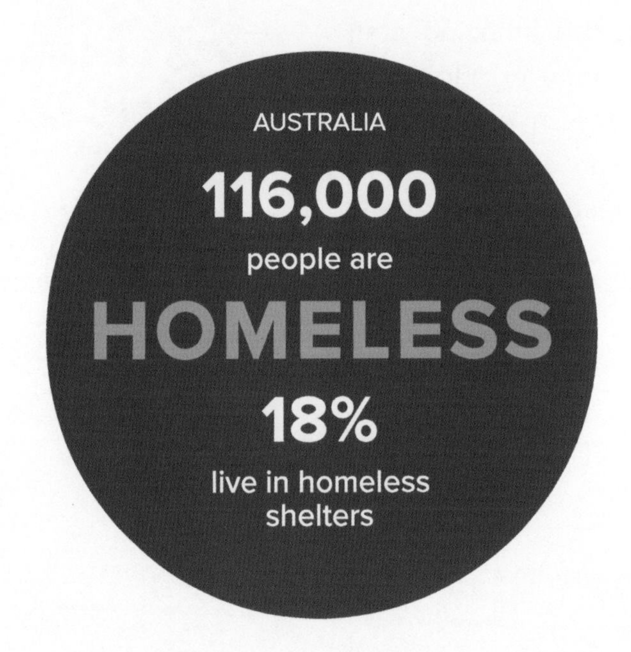
AUSTRALIA
116,000
people are
HOMELESS
18%
live in homeless
shelters

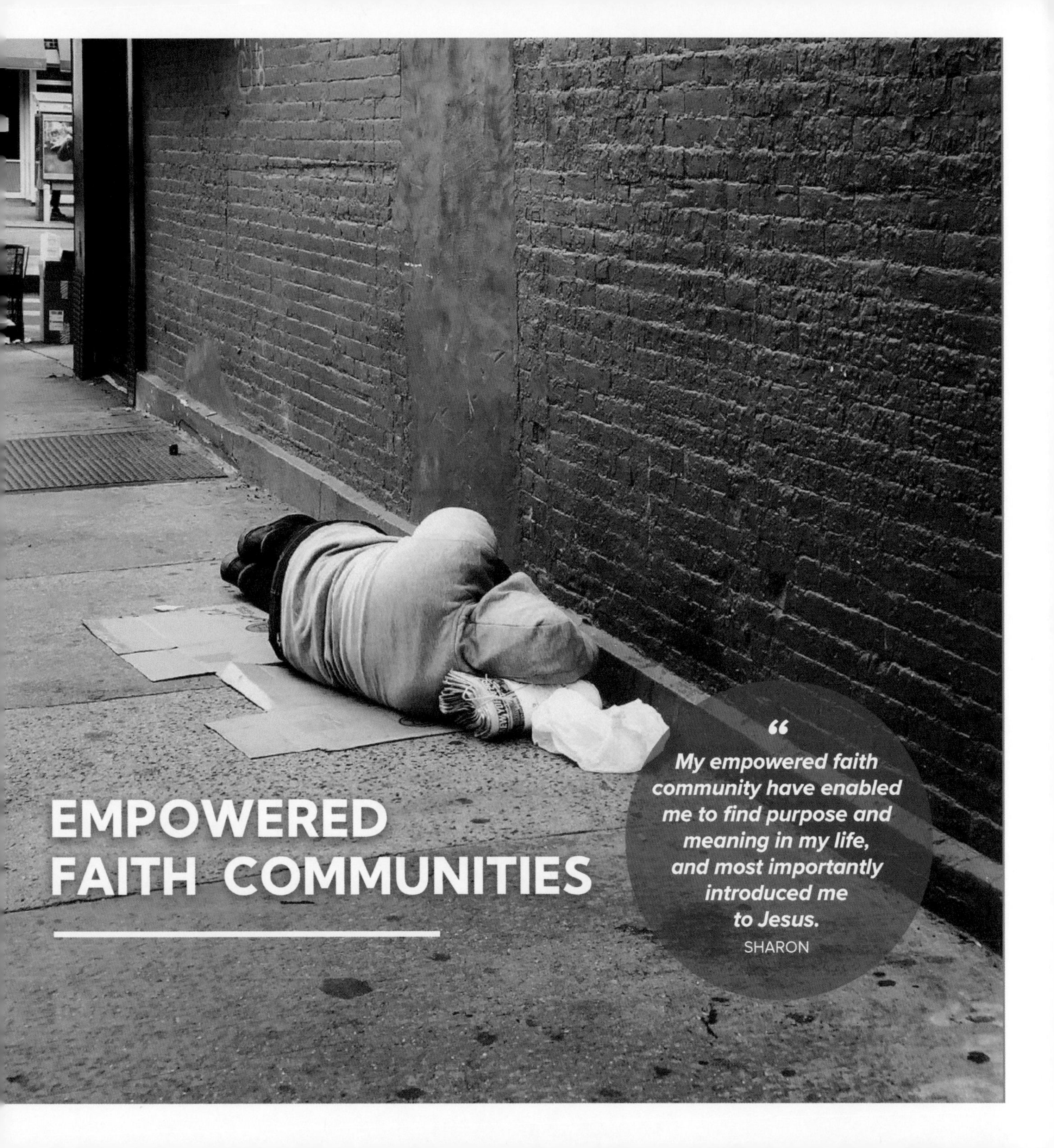

EMPOWERED FAITH COMMUNITIES

> "*My empowered faith community have enabled me to find purpose and meaning in my life, and most importantly introduced me to Jesus.*"
>
> SHARON

EMPOWERED FAITH COMMUNITIES

THE NEED

- In Australia
  - more than 116,000 people are estimated to be homeless. [5]
  - Over 21,000 (18%) living in supported accommodation for the homeless. [5]
  - 8,200 (7%) are rough sleepers. [5]
  - The majority, unknown.
- Homelessness can be caused by poverty, unemployment or it can be triggered by family breakdown, mental illness, sexual assault, addiction, financial difficulty, gambling or social isolation.

THE PROJECT

Empowered Faith Communities helps local churches to build and encourage self-sustaining faith-based communities with those doing life tough.

Being part of a caring, like-minded community is essential for human flourishing The EFC concept centres on community gatherings involving meals with people living in poverty. Utilising community development and discipleship concepts the hope is to see transformation of people within these communities where people can learn to support one another through their hardships together!

INGREDIENTS

- A team of people who are committed to forming relationships with others from a different social space to them
- A resource for providing meals
- Volunteers to serve and prepare meals
- A suitable space to host a weekly or fortnightly gathering
- Attend short orientation meetings with COACH

METHOD

1. Confirm a suitable venue to run the community gatherings
2. Find resources & volunteers to provide meals
3. Recruit a core group of suitable volunteers to run the programme
4. Sign a commitment form for the learning journey with COACH Network
5. Draft a calendar that details the dates and venues of the workshops

HELPING CHURCHES TO BUILD **SELF-SUSTAINING** FAITH BASED **COMMUNITIES** WITH THOSE **DOING LIFE TOUGH**

LIVES TRANSFORMED

"I was struggling to find stable and safe housing. I found myself living in a Caravan Park feeling quite isolated and anxious about moving into a new area with no contacts or social support and no real purpose. The local Baptist Church gave me a food parcel and told me about the Wednesday Night Community Meal. During my journey with the group, I have come to faith in Christ ... I have developed a sense of belonging and purpose in my life."

CAROL

FIND OUT MORE

 *nayba.org/resources/empowered-faith-communities*

 *@EFCAus*

 *@empoweredfaithcommunities*

SOUTH AFRICA

50%

CHILDREN

dont receive sufficient nourishment in their first

one thousand days

SIKUNYE

> "I always thought that growing children was only for mothers, but now I know I am part and parcel of raising young ones and the church should play a vital role.
>
> A BISHOP

SIKUNYE

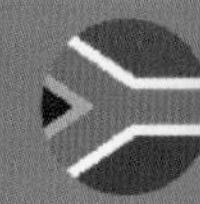

THE NEED

- The First One Thousand Days (from conception to two years) is a once-in-a-life time window of development, in which the brain reaches 80% of it's adult size! [6]
- This crucial period in a child's life is when many foundations are laid for future learning. All children need to consistently receive enough of the right kind of care to realise their full potential.
- Tragically, up to 50% of children in South Africa don't receive enough of the essential building blocks they need in the First Thousand Days of life. [6]

THE PROJECT

Sikunye *(isiXhosa for 'we are together')* helps churches to care for families with children in their First Thousand Days. Through webinars and online resources, churches are equipped to provide the type of support and care that families need so they can ensure that their young children thrive.

All parents need support. When they are doing well, they can provide what their young child needs. Sadly, when they are not doing well, they are not as nurturing or responsive as they need to be. The local church can be the modern-day village around caregivers to see them thrive and their young children reach their God-given potential.

INGREDIENTS

- A sense of calling and commitment to serve families
- Families with children in the First Thousand Days in the church community
- A ministry leader (Champion) to lead activities
- Volunteers in various roles as you implement your activities

METHOD

1. Attend Sikunye's 'The Church & Early Life' webinar to get the big idea
2. Pledge to care for such families
3. Attend Sikunye training workshops to discern your next steps
4. Introduce new initiatives to care for families or tweak what you already have
5. Appoint a lead volunteer to grow the ministry
6. Do, review, learn

HELPING CHURCHES PROVIDE CARE FOR **FAMILIES WITH TODDLERS** IN THEIR **FIRST THOUSAND DAYS**

LIVES TRANSFORMED

"Even before COVID, the First Thousand Days programme at our church was a tremendous blessing to myself and my children.

As the pandemic unveiled itself last year it proved to be even more so. The love and acceptance we have received is reminiscent of family: a close knit, supportive, interceding family... my family within my church family!"

a MUM

FIND OUT MORE

 *nayba.org/resources/sikunye*

 *@sikunye.sa*

 *@sikunye_sa*

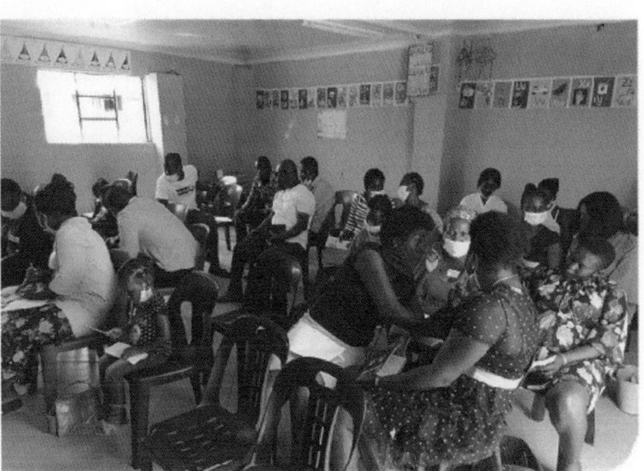

ALBANIA

654

coffeehouses per 100,000 people

CAFE CULTURE

is a way of growing **the 2%** Christian population

UP CAFE

> “When my son or my girls says to me, I'm at Up Cafe, man, I feel good because I know where they are and who they are with.
>
> PARENT

UP CAFE

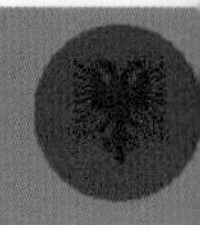

THE NEED

- Coffee and Cafe culture is a way of life in Albania. With 654 coffeehouses per 100,000 inhabitants, Albania is the world leader in the number of coffeehouses per capita. [7]
- Albanians frequent 'cafes' on average 3 times a day to conduct business, work or relax and connect with family and friends. [7]
- Unfortunately many cafe's are not ideal environments for young people.
- Albania is 70% Muslim, and the rest are Catholics and Orthodox, with only 2% being Evangelical Protestants. 'Cafe Culture' is a way for the local church to impact the community. [7]

THE PROJECT

Up Cafe helps the local church to provide a safe attractive place for young people to gather in the heart of the community. By positioning the cafe in an easily accessible place, the cafe is, in effect, bringing God's love into the middle of the neighbourhood.

In Albania the economy is not strong and youth cannot afford to socialise. Even if a young person has no money, at the Up Cafe they are welcome to come and sit and make use of the wifi and socialise. They can feel free and relaxed in the environment and those running the cafe can meet them, start conversations and possibly build friendships.

INGREDIENTS

- Young people and students who like to socialise over coffee
- a project leader with a charismatic personality and a drive to make it work
- an available space in the local community
- to raise sufficient funds to cover start up and running costs for the first year
- sufficient volunteers to help run the operation in the days and hours decided

METHOD

1. Recruit a suitable Cafe Manager
2. Find an attractive venue in the community
3. Draw up a budget and raise the capital
4. Recruit volunteers and run training
5. Acquire all the furniture, fittings and equipment needed
6. Set the hours of operation and make a roster for volunteers & staff
7. Church to provide ongoing pastoral support

HELPING CHURCHES PROVIDE A SAFE ATTRACTIVE PLACE FOR **YOUNG PEOPLE** TO GATHER IN THE **NEIGHBOURHOOD**

LIVES TRANSFORMED

"I went to the manager and said, 'Please, whenever you have a place that my son can work at the Up cafe, just tell me. I just want him to be inside your place. I'm not asking how much you pay him or anything else. I just want him to be in this atmosphere because in that way, I feel sure that my son, my boy, who is 19 years old, is safe.'"

PARENT

FIND OUT MORE

 *nayba.org/resources/up-cafe*

 *@UP-social-coffee*

 *@upsocialcoffeeshkoder*

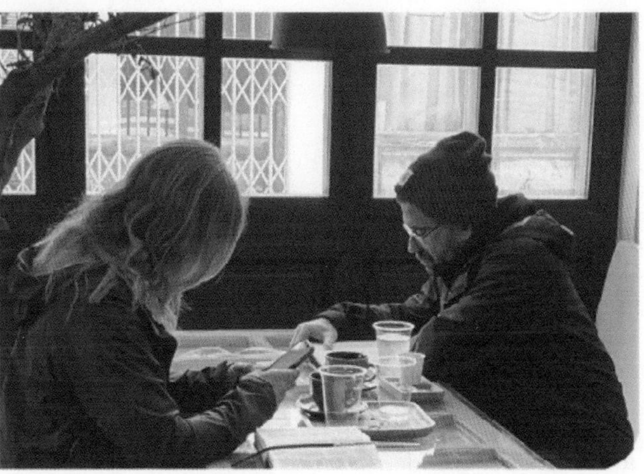

SOUTH AFRICA
has the
3rd Highest
CRIME RATE
in the world
the Police Force are under constant pressure and need community support

ADOPT A **POLICE STATION**

> "We soon discovered that the mandate of the church is similar to the mandate of the police. We both exist for the well-being and protection of our communities
>
> TOPS DE JAGER

ADOPT-A-POLICE STATION

THE NEED

- South Africa has the third-highest crime rate in the world and has a notably high rate of assaults, rape, homicides, and other violent crimes. This has been attributed to several factors, including high levels of poverty, inequality, unemployment, and social exclusion, and the normalization of violence. [8]
- Police officers in South Africa face one of the most daunting crime fighting environments in the world. The scale and scope of crime and restiveness is enough to put immense pressure on SA's 194,605 police officers, all of which is complicated by a complex mix of inequality, disenfranchisement and the legacy of apartheid. [8]

THE PROJECT

Adopt-a-Police Station helps local churches to build a transformational relationship with the leadership and team of their local police station.

This project helps the local church to offer moral, emotional and prayer support to the local police. Also providing practical help including the offer of refurbishing the Police Station and supporting the development of community projects. The partnership creates valuable, meaningful relationships between the church and the police, and ultimately to the reduction in crime and a stronger community.

INGREDIENTS

- Identify your local police station
- Recruit volunteers with a heart for police and community
- Meet and get to know the leadership of the local police station
- Listen to their concerns and needs
- Provide consistent prayer, encouragement and service

METHOD

1. Recruit volunteers who have a heart to serve the police and appoint a Lead Volunteer
2. Mobilise the church to pray for the police
3. Strengthen the church's relationship with the local police station
4. Find out how the church can best serve them
5. Serve through a chaplaincy, a prayer line or refurbishing buildings and any other ways
6. Track crime reduction and community cohesion

HELPING CHURCHES TO BUILD GENUINE RELATIONSHIPS WITH THE LEADERSHIP AND TEAM OF THEIR **LOCAL POLICE STATION**

LIVES TRANSFORMED

"There is often an uneasy relationship between a community and their local police force. A few years ago our church in Pretoria started getting involved in a partnership with our local police station.

We found that by building a Community Police Partnership and empowering our church to take hands and support the local police spiritually, emotionally and physically, resulted in a safer community - and it was also an incredible way to show God's love."

VOLUNTEER

FIND OUT MORE

 *nayba.org/resources/adoptapolicestation*

 *@doxadeoparkview*

 *@doxadeoparkview*

GLOBALLY

12 million

people are incarcerated in

PRISONS

which are grossly

overcrowded

in 50% of all countries

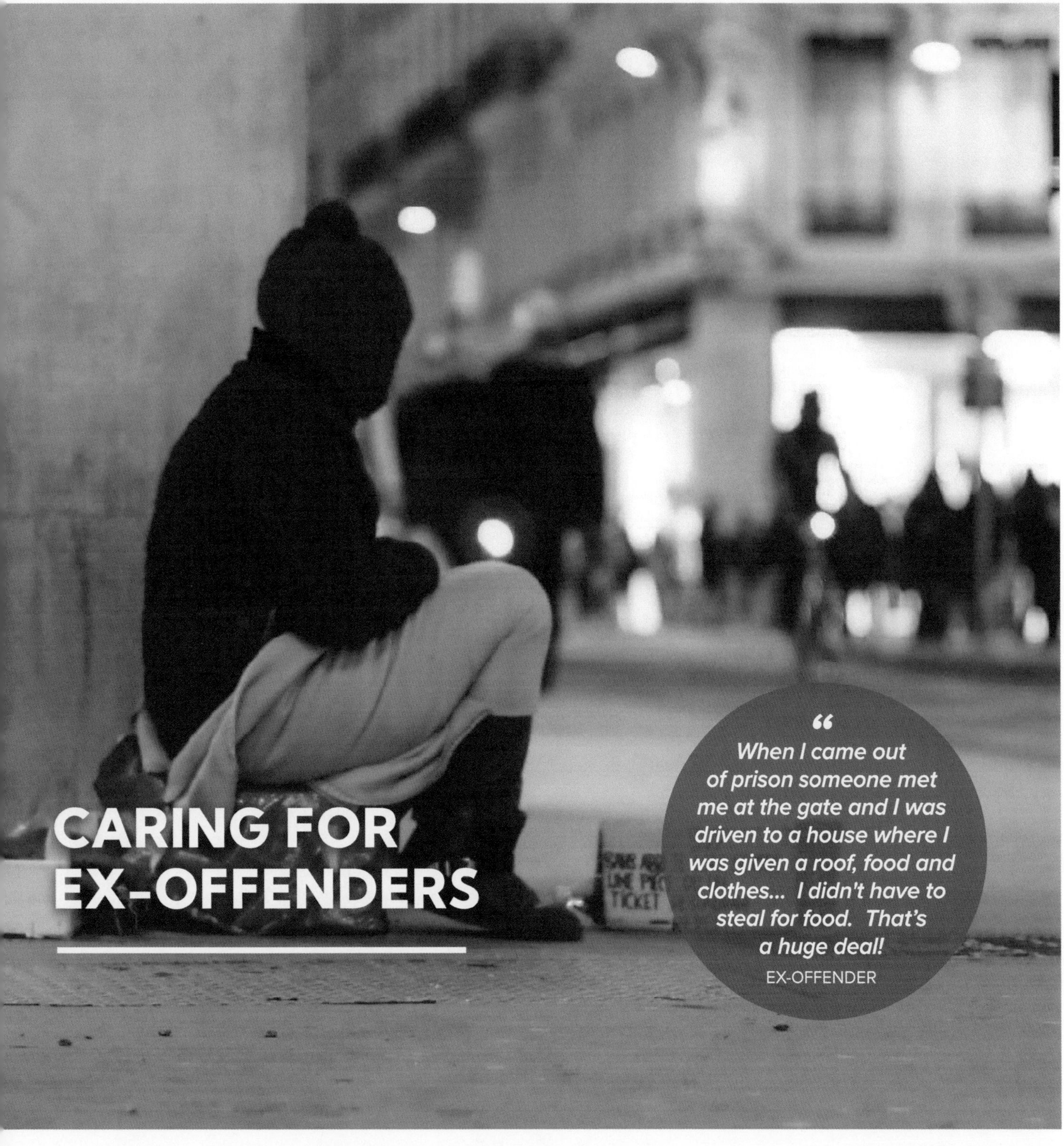

CARING FOR EX-OFFENDERS

"When I came out of prison someone met me at the gate and I was driven to a house where I was given a roof, food and clothes... I didn't have to steal for food. That's a huge deal!

EX-OFFENDER

CARING FOR EX-OFFENDERS

THE NEED

- Australia has over 36,000 prisoners and spends more than $2.6 billion AUS per year to keep them in there. [9]
- A third of ex-inmates spend their first night out of jail sleeping rough or homeless. [9]
- The re-conviction rate within a year of release can be as high as 76%. [9]
- Many female prisoners ore victims of some form of abuse, and over 40 per cent are homeless upon release. [9]
- The children of prisoners are six times more likely to be imprisoned themselves. [9]

THE PROJECT

Caring for Ex-Offenders (CFEO) helps local churches to reduce crime by reintegrating ex-offenders into the community. CFEO equips churches, through training and mentorship, enabling them to provide support to ex-offenders and help them live transformed lives.

To support those coming out of Prison the CFEO network trains communities to care for ex-offenders. These communities will meet someone coming out of prison at the gate and provide mentoring, friendship and practical support such as accommodation and help with job training and employment.

INGREDIENTS

- Identify a passion and a need to care for ex-offenders in the local community
- Marshal a committed and compassionate group of church volunteers
- Attend a free half day training workshop, either online or face-to-face
- Access free training materials online
- Establish contact with a WW State Co-Ordinator and obtain guidance and support

METHOD

1. Identify and select prospective volunteers
2. Contact a William Wilberforce State Co-Ordinator via the website
3. Complete an in-depth guided risk evaluation
4. Agree a suitable date for free training
5. Access free on-line training materials
6. Liaise with the State Co-Ordinator to select and match the appropriate mentor. This could be 12 months before the release date

LIVES TRANSFORMED

"I first met Don in Jail. I wasn't shore wat to expect or how he could help as my life started in a broken home with violence and abuse. I had spent over 12 years in Jail. Anyway I agreed to let Don pick me up upon my release. I was so nervous and anxious with all that was going on but Don helped me through everything. He went above and beyond not only driving me around but helped me mentally and also understood were I was coming from."

KEN

FIND OUT MORE

 *nayba.org/resources/caringforexoffenders*

 *@wilberforcefoundation*

 *@williamwilberforcefoundation*

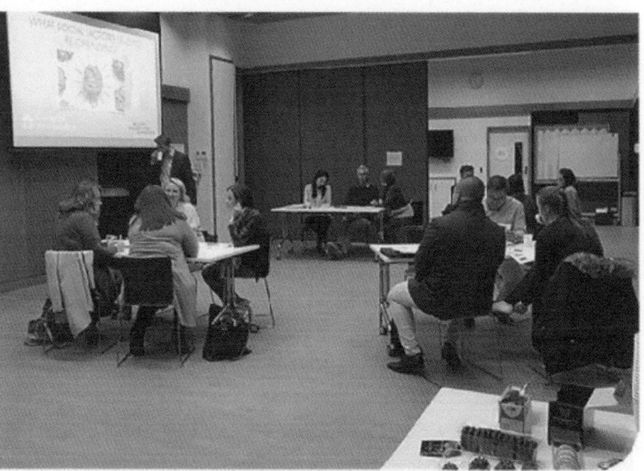

SOUTH AFRICA

2.13 million

children are effectively

FATHERLESS

9 million

grow up without fathers
In their homes

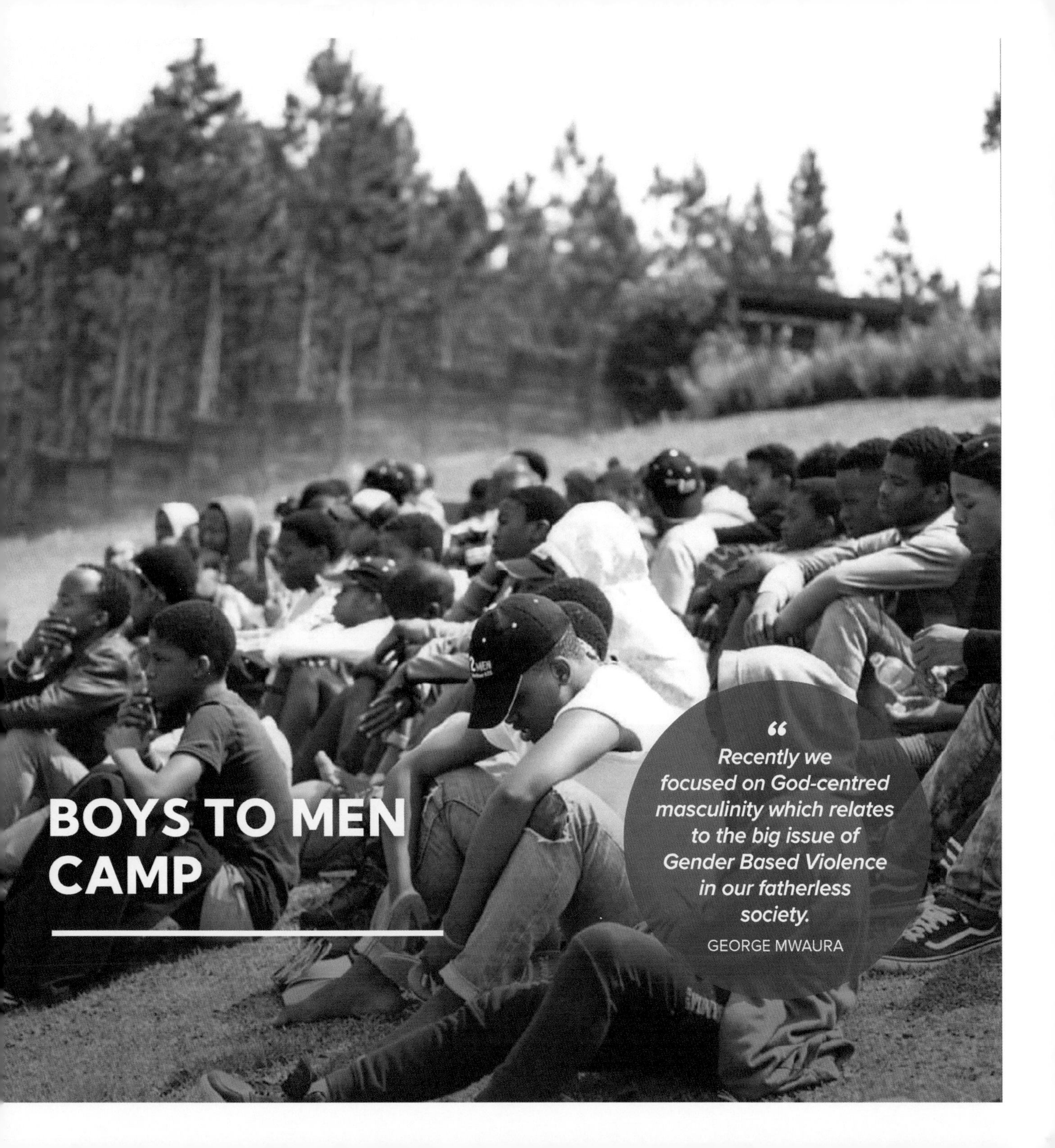

BOYS TO MEN CAMP

> *"Recently we focused on God-centred masculinity which relates to the big issue of Gender Based Violence in our fatherless society.*
>
> GEORGE MWAURA

BOYS TO MEN CAMP

THE NEED

- In a report released in February 2021, StatsSA revealed that most "children in South Africa live in non-standard family structures with mostly only one of their biological parents."
- Over 2 million children in South Africa are effectively fatherless, and 9 million grow-up without fathers present in their homes, a tremendous fatherhood challenge for the country; [10]
- Generally on Boys to Men Camps it is found that 75% of the boys come from homes with no fathers and 15% of the remaining 25% come from homes with absent fathers.

THE PROJECT

The **Boys To Men** camp helps local churches in South Africa impact young boys as they transition into manhood. This church project came about as a response to the overwhelming need that many South African boys face to have active father figures in their lives.

Since 2010, Boys to Men has been providing tools to churches to host theme-based camps for young boys at a crucial stage in their lives, with the aim of breaking the cycle of fatherlessness in our society.

INGREDIENTS

- A community of young boys needing mentorship
- A lead volunteer with the necessary credentials and experience
- Volunteer helpers who can be trained
- An equipped and secure camping facility within close proximity
- To gather the necessary resources including transport, food and recreational equipment

METHOD

1. Receive training tools from Boys 2 Men
2. Facilitate training of all helpers
3. Secure the use of a suitable camping ground in the local area
4. Recruit camp participants
5. Plan and execute the camp programme
6. Follow up with ongoing friendship and pastoral support for camp attendees

HELPING CHURCHES IN SOUTH AFRICA TO IMPACT **YOUNG BOYS** AS THEY TRANSITION INTO **MANHOOD**

LIVES TRANSFORMED

"I was very depressed, insecure and had a lot of problems I had to face until boys to men came into my life and gave me the tools to deal with them.

They welcomed me with open arms and showed me what love and appreciation is, they helped me accept myself for who and what I am without any judgement. They even helped me find myself and I discovered things about me that I never even knew I had. And for all that I have a great appreciation and respect for the organization"

JORDAN

FIND OUT MORE

 *nayba.org/resources/boystomen*

 *@CASTngo*

 *@cast_ngo*

MATERIAL

GLOBALLY

55 million

people are internally

DISPLACED

due to conflict, disaster and domestic breakdown

excluding refugees

DE RUSTPLEK

> *I hear the doorbell and there is Samir with a few things... I take him to his room to settle in. Walking downstairs to make coffee makes me feel grateful that we can be his resting place.*
>
> A RUSPTPLEK HOST

DE RUST PLEK

THE NEED

- The need for shelter for people in crisis is increasing. The number of internally displaced people across the globe reached 55 million by the end of 2020, with 40.5 million new displacements, the highest annual figure recorded in a decade. [11]
- As of 31 December 2020, worldwide, there were more than double internally displaced people than refugees. Note that this was prior to the war in Ukraine. [11]
- Housing provides people with dignity and the opportunity to lead a normal life. Shelter plays an essential role in reducing vulnerability and building resilience.

THE PROJECT

De Rustplek *(The Resting Place)* - helps the local church to assist people who find themselves in crisis situations by offering temporary shelter in private homes in the community.

A local church in the Netherlands identified a need in their community for people in crisis to find shelter. A number of host families volunteered to offer a room in their homes for a couple of weeks or months, giving social workers in the community time to work with those in crisis to find a solution.

This is a way for preventing escalating problems in families and to help individuals not to slip into homelessness.

INGREDIENTS

- Individuals and families in crisis
- A lead volunteer who is a gifted facilitator
- A system for recruiting host families
- Host families who are willing to offer a room in their home for temporary shelter
- Social counselling professionals in the community willing to volunteer their services
- Pastoral support for the lead volunteers and the people in crisis

METHOD

1. Recruit a lead volunteer
2. Undertake Resting Place training.
3. Secure an online platform for recruiting host volunteers
4. Recruit professionals who can assist through counselling and practical care
5. Recruit those in need through relationships and referrals
6. Ongoing pastoral support for those in crisis

HELPING CHURCHES ASSIST **PEOPLE IN CRISIS** BY OFFERING **TEMPORARY SHELTER** IN PRIVATE HOMES

LIVES TRANSFORMED

"I found a spot and I'm happy with it! Because a bed to sleep in is so much better than spending the night in my car. I don't think the night work I do is ideal for the family I stay with... soon I decide to quit my night shift and it was such a relief. I notice I need time to recover from everything I've been through. Soon my supervisor finds me a new job. Now weekends can be weekends again; resting, cleaning my room and doing laundry. I'm starting to find my rhythm, and am grateful for this place."

SAMIR

FIND OUT MORE

 *nayba.org/resources/derustplek*

 *@derustplek*

 *@derustplek*

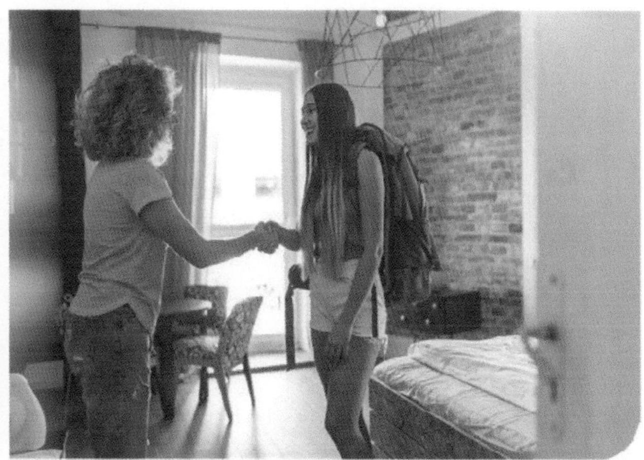

AUSTRALIA

3.6 million

people experience levels of

FOOD INSECURITY

48%

of those are are employed

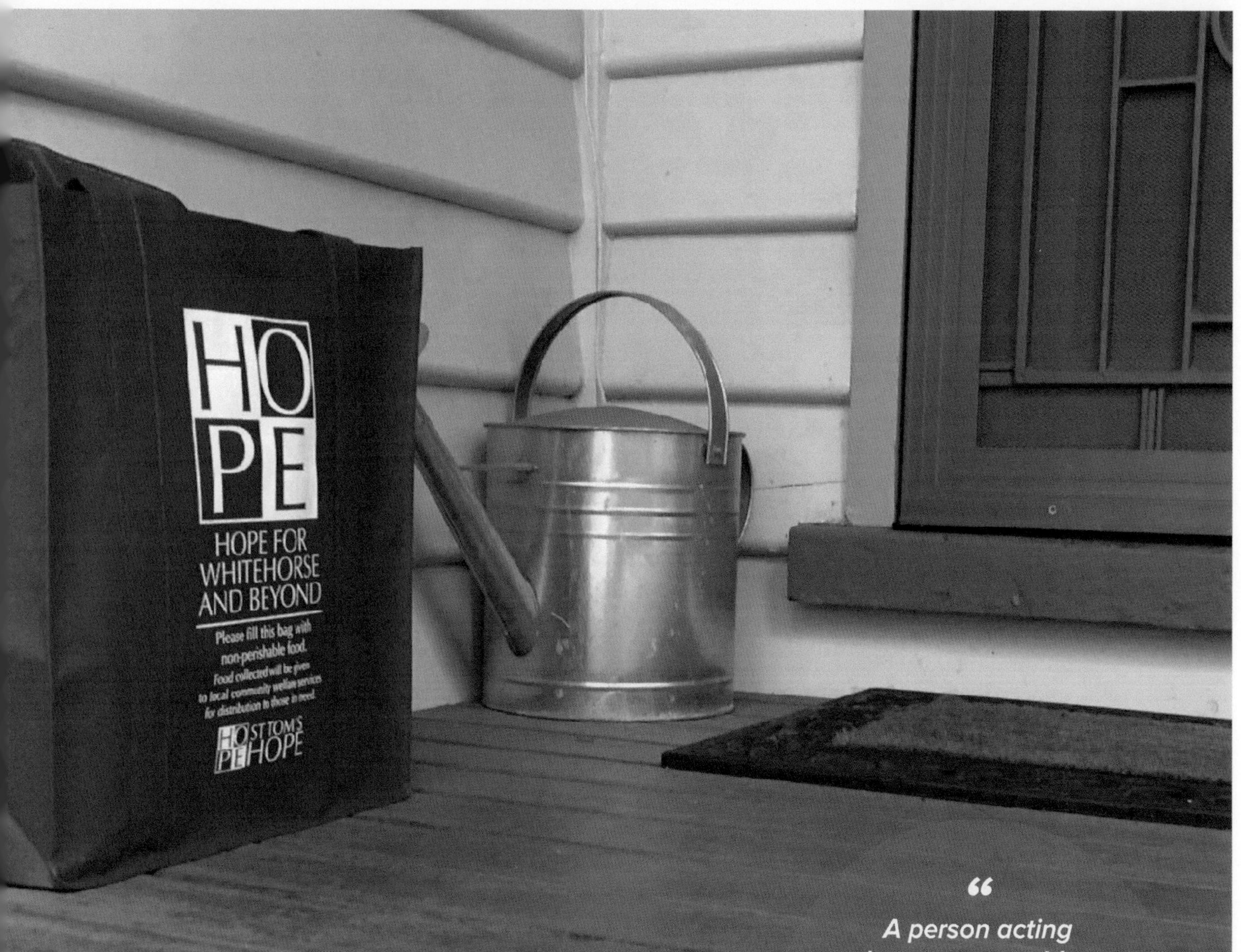

HOPE FILLED BAGS

> "A person acting alone cannot achieve a lot but when many people act together and pool their various skills and talents a great deal can be done.
>
> GIL MUIR

HOPE FILLED BAGS

THE NEED

- Food insecurity is defined as "a situation that exists when people lack secure access to sufficient amounts of safe and nutritious food for normal growth and development".
- In 2021 3.6 million Australians (15%) experienced food insecurity at least once in the year. Three in five of these individuals experience food insecurity at least once a month. [12]
- Food insecurity is not restricted to the unemployed or homeless, as 48% of food insecure Australians are employed in some way, whether full-time, part-time or casually. [12]
- Dependent children live in 40% of food insecure households. [12]

THE PROJECT

Hope Filled Bags helps local churches to respond to food insecurity in their community.

A church running the project provides its members with the Hope grocery bags who distribute these to their family, friends, neighbours and others who are motivated to donate grocery items to those in the community who are living tough.

The Hope Filled Bags are returned by the happy donors and the donation is then brought to the church where it is delivered to the local Food Bank or another local community service organisation.

INGREDIENTS

- A need for food relief services in your area
- Compassionate church members excited to donate food using Hope Filled Bags
- A coordinator who will oversee the project
- Hope Bags ordered or locally sourced
- Set dates for hand out and return of bags to church members
- Organise the delivery of the donations to local food relief services

METHOD

1. Launch the idea in your church community and obtain support
2. Order a supply of Hope Bags
3. Appeal to church members to take a number of bags, to distribute to friends
4. Invite people in the community to participate
5. Arrange with a local supermarket to set up a stall on a Saturday morning to gain support

HELPING CHURCHES RESPOND TO **FOOD INSECURITY** IN THEIR COMMUNITY

LIVES TRANSFORMED

"Just want to express my gratitude for all the efforts of your organisation to help the international students like me. This is priceless and means a lot to me. You have influenced me to be more helpful and concerned for others. Keep on inspiring!"

INTERNATIONAL STUDENT

FIND OUT MORE

 *nayba.org/resources/hopefilledbags*

 *@stthomashope*

 *@stthomashope*

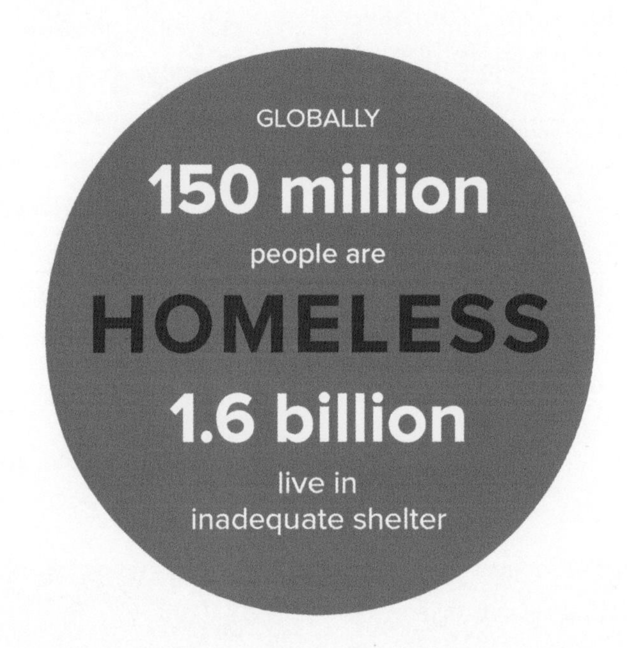
GLOBALLY
150 million
people are
HOMELESS
1.6 billion
live in
inadequate shelter

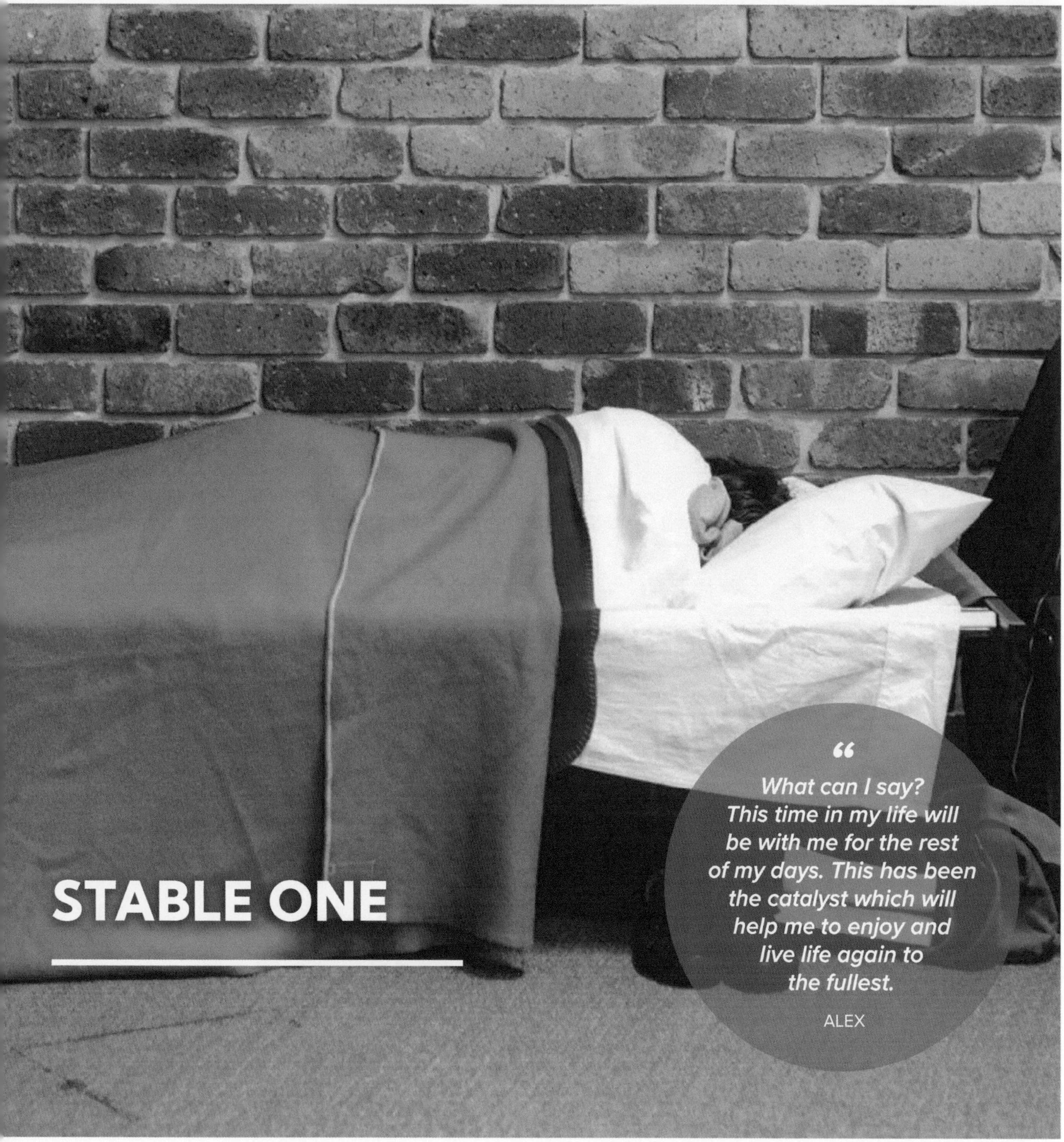

STABLE ONE

> “What can I say? This time in my life will be with me for the rest of my days. This has been the catalyst which will help me to enjoy and live life again to the fullest.
>
> ALEX

STABLE ONE

THE NEED

- It is estimated that 150 million people are homeless worldwide. Habitat for Humanity estimated in 2016 that 1.6 billion people around the world live in "inadequate shelter". [13]
- Different countries use different definitions of homelessness. It can be defined by living in a shelter, being in a transitional phase of housing and living in a place not fit for human habitation.
- Over 116,000 Australians and 24,000 residents of Victoria will be homeless tonight. [13]
- They include families with children, young and older people, single adults and people with disabilities. [13]

THE PROJECT

Stable One helps local churches in a region work together to provide care and shelter for the most vulnerable in their communities.

Offering safe and supportive shelter for those experiencing, or at risk of homelessness, Stable One is resourcing the Church to work together across denominations to care for the most vulnerable in our communities.

A Winter Shelter typically runs for 13 weeks from June to August and provides a powerful opportunity for churches and volunteers to connect with the reality of homelessness in their neighbourhoods.

INGREDIENTS

- An unmet need in the local area to provide for people experiencing homelessness
- A Project Co-ordinator who is passionate about Jesus and people
- 7 local churches willing to work together
- A trailer and 10 sets of bedding
- A robust prayer team
- Volunteers (around 150)
- Funding / Sponsorships

METHOD

1. Invite Winter Shelter network to speak at an open meeting of local churches
2. Appoint a Winter Shelter Project Co-ordinator
3. Agree governance structure
4. Gain commitment from 7 local churches to each take responsibility one night per week
5. Undertake Winter Shelter training
6. Build relationships with local services, relief organisations, hospitals, police and other

HELPING CHURCHES IN A REGION WORK TOGETHER TO PROVIDE **CARE AND SHELTER** FOR THE MOST VULNERABLE

LIVES TRANSFORMED

"It all started off as a marriage breakdown. Things just got bad and I felt like I had sort of no one to turn to. Ended up on the street living pretty rough for many years. One day the people from the Winter Shelter showed up and invited me to join. At first I boycotted it a little bit - I was just so down and out and and suddenly there's people trying to help and I'm thinking what's the catch? Just being able to sit down at a table and have a meal with someone else, you know, it was a really big thing and having a bed after being on the streets for seven years is something that I wasn't used to. To be honest, it's the Winter Shelter that helped save me life."

CLAYTON HOOK

FIND OUT MORE

 *nayba.org/resources/stableone*

@StableOneMoreThanAPlaceToStay

 *@stableone_australia*

GUERNSEY

3,000
households
live in
POVERTY
including
single parents
& **pensioners**

GUERNSEY WELFARE CENTRE

"

Lovely friendly people — always there when you need them!

JULIE

GUERNSEY WELFARE CENTRE

THE NEED

- There's no doubt about it, Guernsey in the Channel Islands is a wonderful place to live - but behind closed doors there's another picture for some.
- Currently over 3,000 households (16%) in Guernsey are poor. People in these households have a low income and suffer from multiple deprivation. [14]
- 63% of single parents have a low income whilst 43% of single pensioners also live in poverty. [14]

THE PROJECT

Guernsey Welfare Centre helps a group of local churches on the island by providing a central venue which offers hospitality and a refuge for those who are in need.

The Welfare Centre is supported by many denominations of churches in both practical and prayerful ways, and offers a number of community services including:

- A Food Bank which is open five days a week;
- Ablution facilities with a shower, and washing machines for the homeless;
- Internet access for the unemployed or those looking for somewhere to live;
- A Community Cafe - a hub of hospitality where the vulnerable can enjoy a cup of tea and a chat;
- A Linking LIves scheme which helps to link up volunteers with elderly isolated people;

INGREDIENTS

- An attractive venue easily accessible to the community
- A range of appealing services aimed at meeting the unique needs of the local community - such as hunger, joblessness and loneliness amongst the elderly
- A team of volunteers inspired to serve
- A website and social media pages to assist in communicating with the local community

METHOD

1. Bring together a group of local churches united in their quest to help their community
2. Find an accessible / practical / venue
3. Register a Charity with local government, which may qualify you to receive a social welfare grant
4. Set-up a governance structure including a leadership committee
5. Set-up a fund raising committee

HELPING CHURCHES TO WORK TOGETHER TO PROVIDE A CENTRE OFFERING **REFUGE** FOR THOSE WHO ARE **IN NEED**

LIVES TRANSFORMED

"One of the exciting initiatives we've been involved in recently has been the development of a Welfare Centre which is supported by many denominations of churches on the Island including Baptist, Church of England, Methodist, New Frontiers, Catholics and Salvation Army in both practical and prayerful.

We're very excited about the potential that this place has and we hope that we can use it to provide hospitality and a refuge for those who are in need."

REV JON HONOUR

FIND OUT MORE

 *nayba.org/resources/guernseywelfare*

 *@Guernsey-Welfare-Service*

 *@guernseywelfare*

AFRICA

460 million

live in

EXTREME POVERTY

which is the continent's

biggest challenge

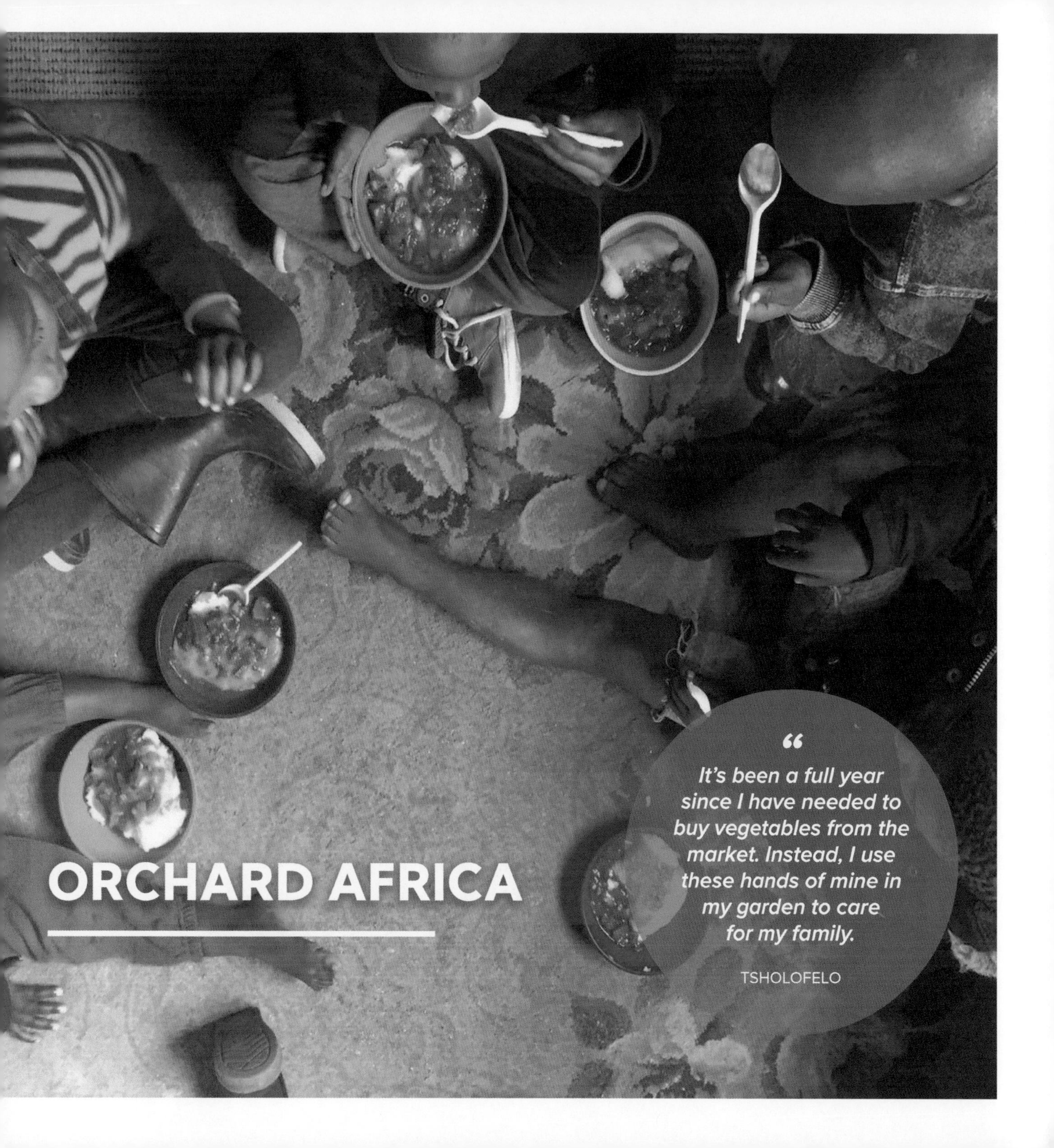

ORCHARD AFRICA

> *“It’s been a full year since I have needed to buy vegetables from the market. Instead, I use these hands of mine in my garden to care for my family.*
>
> TSHOLOFELO

ORCHARD AFRICA

THE NEED

- While the richest Africans get ever richer, extreme poverty in the continent is rising. Africa is the second most unequal continent in the world, and home to seven of the most unequal countries.
- In 2022, around 460 million people in Africa were living in extreme poverty, with the poverty threshold at 1.90 U.S. dollars a day. [15]

THE PROJECT

Orchard Africa helps local churches to respond in practical ways to poverty in their communities, by equipping them through relief, reconstruction and development programmes.

- The Food & Agriculture programme emphasizes food security by providing meals and teaching communities to grow their own food.
- The Education programme helps local churches start a preschool, provide an after-school learning center, and conduct life skills and entrepreneurial training for older students.
- The Care programme equips church leaders to be the hands and feet of Jesus through home-based care, trauma counseling, HIV/AIDS prevention, and orphan intervention.
- The Ministry programme focuses on training, mentoring, and equipping local African pastors and their churches to respond to the immediate needs of their own community.

INGREDIENTS

- An unmet need in the local area to respond to poverty and injustice
- A Project Co-ordinator who is passionate about helping people
- Local churches willing to work together
- A strategy for rolling out the most relevant programme for the region
- Skilled and unskilled volunteers with a heart to help

METHOD

1. Register on the Orchard Africa website and find all information about becoming a partner
2. meet with local churches and assess the unique needs of the area
3. Appoint a Project Co-ordinator
4. Undertake Orchard Africa training
5. Embark on the roll-out of the first programme and evaluate

LIVES TRANSFORMED

"One woman shared that because of the gift of a warm blanket and a hot water bottle, she can brave the bitter cold at night and attend her church prayer meeting. These two small gifts provides her not only with warmth but also with the opportunity for spiritual growth and an evening of fellowship with her church community."

MICHELLE TESSENDORF

FIND OUT MORE

 *nayba.org/resources/orchardafrica*

 *@OrchardAfrica*

 *@OrchardAfrica*

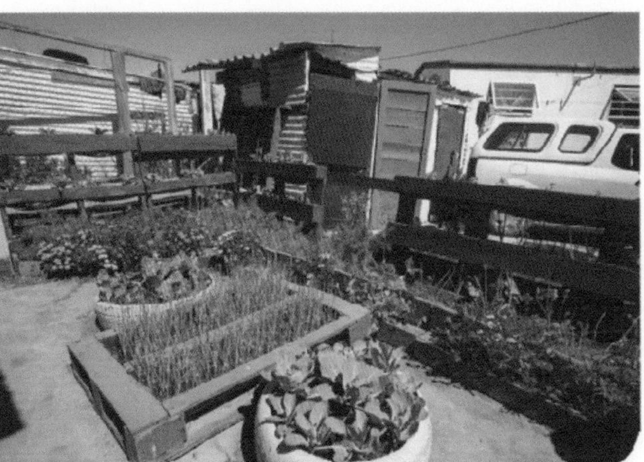

GLOBALLY

65%

people suffer

FINANCIAL STRESS

made worse by the

global pandemic

COMMUNITY FOOD CARE

> "They do such an incredible job helping people in our communities to live better lives.
>
> A MUM

COMMUNITY FOOD CARE

THE NEED

- Nearly 900,000 people in New South Wales, Australia live below the poverty line. [16]
- More than one in six children across the state are living in poverty. [16]
- Women are more likely to experience disadvantage than men. [16]

THE PROJECT

Community FoodCare helps local churches to provide assistance to people and families who are struggling financially.

The programme provides grocery hampers for a nominal service and handling fee along with free fruit, vegetables and bread weekly to every family and individual with a concession benefit card who are facing a crisis or financial hardship.

The project has a proven system of operation that can easily be shared with a local church. it also has relationships with food suppliers and councils, which will help churches with food supply and civic support.

Community FoodCare exists to give you a helping hand when you need it the most.

INGREDIENTS

- People who are struggling financially in the community.
- A lead volunteer
- A secure room where food can be stored
- Storage equipment including a fridge, freezer and shelving
- People willing to donate food items
- Team of volunteers

METHOD

1. Contact Community Foodcare - find out more
2. Recruit lead volunteer and team
3. Undergo training with Community Foodcare
4. Set up a secure refrigerated storage room
5. Mobilise church to provide initial stock of food
6. Advertise service to community and service providers and attend community events
7. Volunteers create weekly food hampers for the required size of the household

HELPING CHURCHES TO PROVIDE FOOD TO PEOPLE AND FAMILIES WHO ARE **STRUGGLING FINANCIALLY**

LIVES TRANSFORMED

"Before a friend recommended Foodcare to me, I had $10 a fortnight left over for food and could only afford to eat toast. I would go to my parents for a meal a couple of times a week. I also started going to church more often because parishioners would bring in leftover fruit from their fruit trees and I could take as much as I liked. Community Foodcare has made me feel more independent with a much more balanced and healthy diet."

A YOUNG WOMAN

FIND OUT MORE

 *nayba.org/resources/communityfoodcare*

 *@BayCityCareCommunityFoodCare*

WELLBEING

GLOBALLY

20%

of women suffer from

BROKENESS

mental health issues such as

Anxiety and
Depression

PEACED TOGETHER

> "Peaced Together has helped me to look again at the broken areas of my life and find fresh hope for the future."
>
> NAOMI

PEACED TOGETHER

THE NEED

- One in five women have a common mental health problem such as depression and anxiety.
- Women are twice as likely to be diagnosed with anxiety as men. [17]
- 26% of young women aged between 16–24 years old report having common mental health problems in any given week. This compares to 17% of all adults. [17]
- 53% of women who have mental health problems have also experienced abuse. [17]
- 1.6 million women in England and Wales experienced domestic abuse in 2021. [17]

THE PROJECT

Peaced Together helps local churches work with women who have experienced brokenness or difficult circumstances, helping them restore their lives through a creative arts course with a difference.

Believing that good can come from negative and difficult experiences, the 10 week course uses five themed craft projects, encouraging women to reflect on their lives and set out on a personal journey from brokenness to hope.

The five craft projects are completed over the ten weeks and each project helps the group explore topics such as beauty, peace with the past and positive choices.

INGREDIENTS

- Women needing restoration
- A lead volunteer who is a gifted facilitator
- Two team members interested in crafts
- A meeting space
- Craft materials and tools
- Pastoral support for the volunteers course participants of the course

METHOD

1. Recruit a lead volunteer and team
2. Undertake Peaced Together training
3. Secure the use of a meeting space, tables & chairs suitable for creative activities
4. Obtain craft materials and tools
5. Recruit course participants
6. Deliver the course

HELPING CHURCHES WORK WITH **WOMEN** EXPERIENCING **BROKENNESS** - BRINGING **RESTORATION** TO THEIR LIVES

LIVES TRANSFORMED

"Before I did the Peaced Together course I didn't like myself. I never thought I could be good at crafts or anything for that matter. And then I realised that I could sew! Learning new skills made me think that maybe I could try new things. I realised I could make anything I wanted if I put my mind to it. I look at life so differently now, I don't look at the bad stuff. You can make new things from old. I accept myself now and I don't beat myself up about things. I still struggle with depression sometimes, but I handle it better now."

MARCIA

FIND OUT MORE

 *nayba.org/resources/peacedtogether*

 *@beautyfrombrokeness*

 *@peaced.together1*

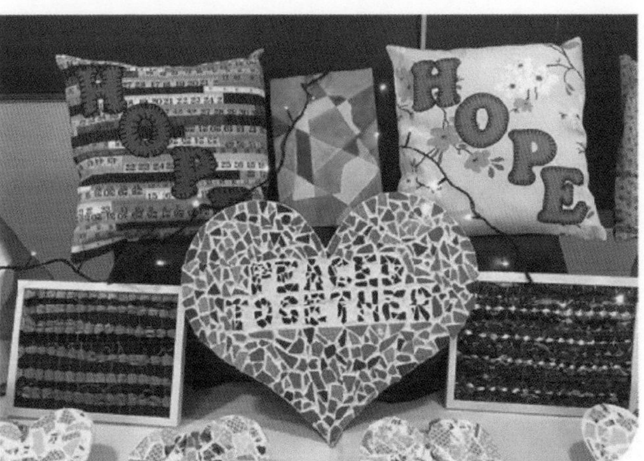

GLOBALLY

107.5 million

Alcohol use Disorders

ADDICTION

35 million

Substance Abuse Disorders

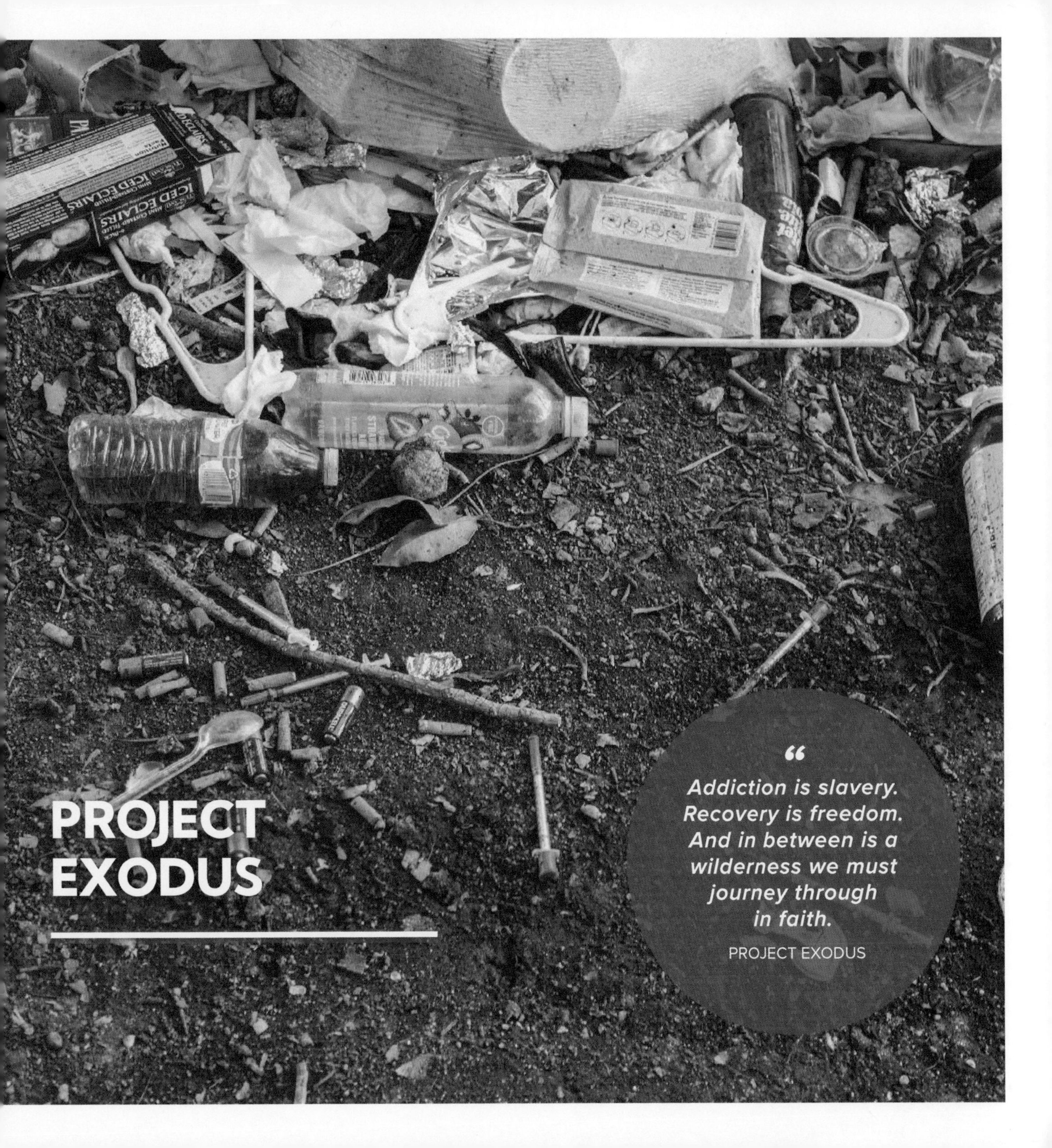
ICED ECLAIRS
ICED ECLAIRS
PROJECT EXODUS
"Addiction is slavery. Recovery is freedom. And in between is a wilderness we must journey through in faith.
PROJECT EXODUS

PROJECT EXODUS

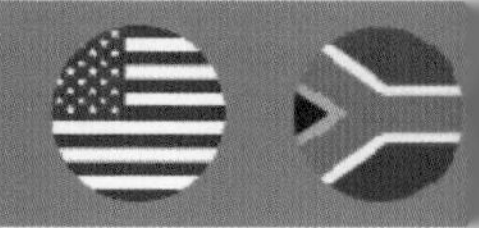

THE NEED

Globally addiction is a social crisis indiscriminately affecting people of all nations, ages, genders, races, and cultures. The following numbers indicate the extent of the global battle with addiction:

- 107,5 million Alcohol Use Disorders. [18]
- 35 million Substance Abuse Disorders. [18]
- 23 million addicted to Gaming. [18]

THE PROJECT

Project Exodus helps local churches journey with those caught in addiction through evidence based recovery programmes.

Seven out of every eight people that require addiction treatment never receive the help they so desperately need. Through Project Exodus, a paradigm shift is created in order to radically change this statistic.

Project Exodus uses innovative and ground-breaking strategies to address issues of substance dependence, pornography addiction and other compulsive disorders in resolution-orientated ways.

INGREDIENTS

- A project leader with a heart to set the captives free
- A committed church leadership
- A willingness to drive ongoing awareness of addiction within the community
- Participate in the Exodus Recovery Skills (ERS) training programme

METHOD

1. Contact Project Exodus (PEx) to indicate interest and discuss next steps
2. Sign a commitment to honour the PEx intellectual property
3. Receive access to the PEx resources needed
4. Participate in the 16-week ERS Facilitator Training Programme
5. Launch your recovery group with the guidance of the PEx support team

HELPING CHURCHES JOURNEY WITH THOSE **CAUGHT** IN **ADDICTION** THROUGH A UNIQUE **RECOVERY** PROGRAMME

LIVES TRANSFORMED

"Project Exodus has been a life-changer for me. When I look back to who I was 12 months ago, I cannot recognise the person I used to be. Highly recommended!"

ERS OUTPATIENT

FIND OUT MORE

 *nayba.org/resources/projectexodus*

 *@projectexodusrecovery*

 *@projectexodusrecovery*

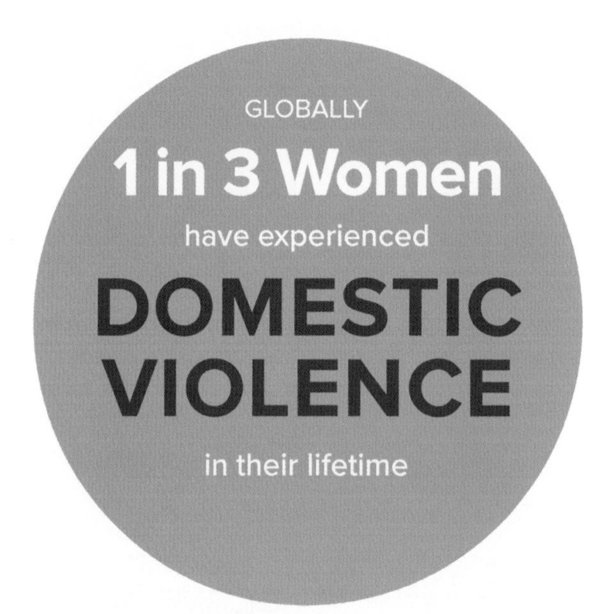
GLOBALLY
1 in 3 Women
have experienced
DOMESTIC
VIOLENCE
in their lifetime

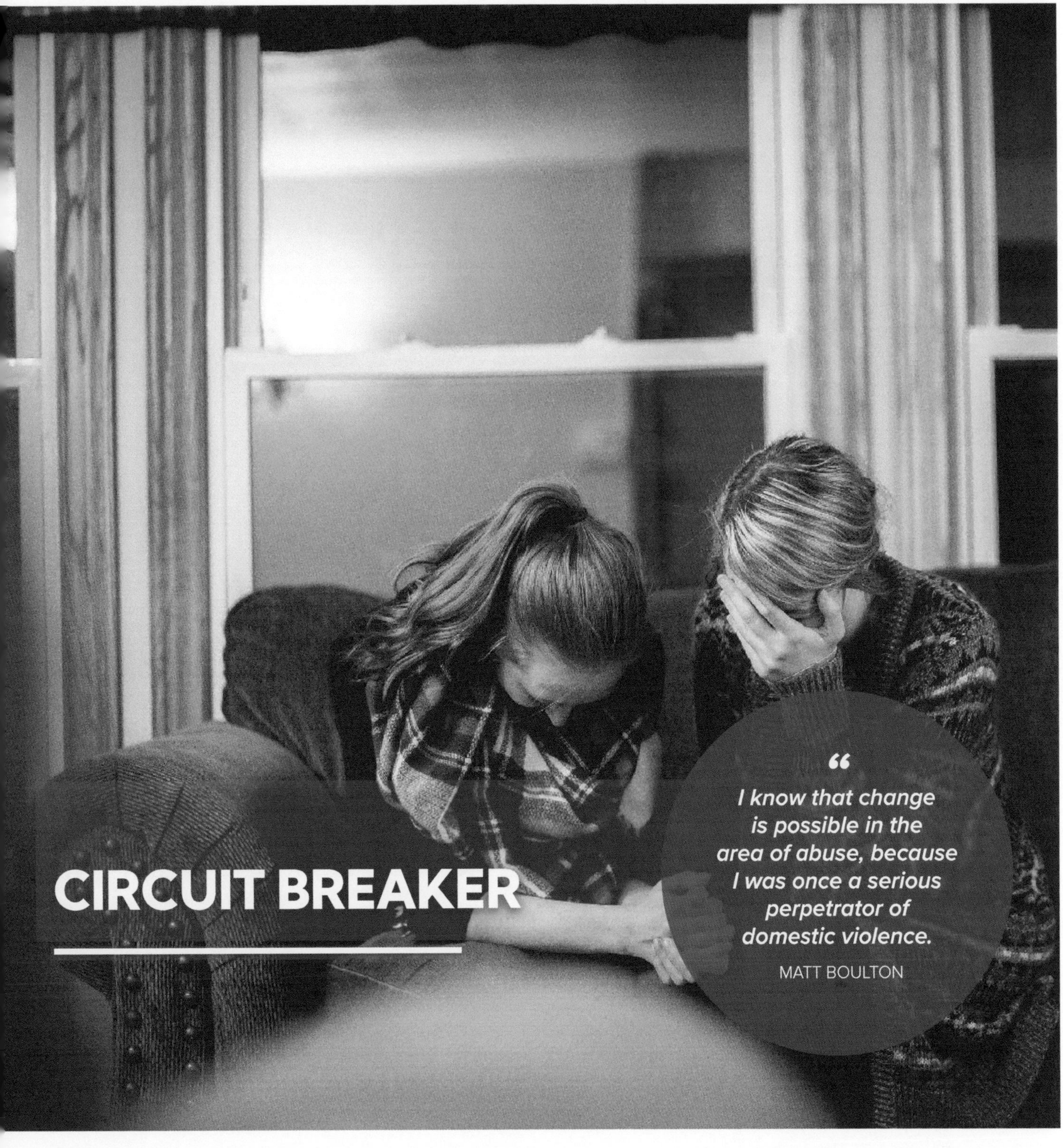

CIRCUIT BREAKER

> "I know that change is possible in the area of abuse, because I was once a serious perpetrator of domestic violence.
>
> MATT BOULTON

CIRCUIT BREAKER

THE NEED

- Globally about 1 in 3 women worldwide have been subjected to either physical and/or sexual partner violence or non-partner violence in their lifetime. [19]
- Fewer than 40% of the women who experience violence seek help of any sort. Among women who do, fewer than 10% seek help by appealing to the police. [19]
- Violence can negatively affect a person's physical, mental, sexual, and reproductive health, and may increase the risk of acquiring HIV in some settings.

THE PROJECT

The **Circuit Breaker Course** equips local churches to help prevent domestic violence in their communities. The course resources volunteers to be able to find meaningful engagement with potential perpetrators of domestic violence.

Circuit Breaker provides a full ten-week package that any local church can use. The course has manuals and teaching videos, which means that volunteer group facilitators do not need to be teachers or counsellors.

Circuit Breaker hopes to reach domestic violence before it begins, by using an army of local church volunteers, equipped by the course.

INGREDIENTS

- Compassionate Church Volunteers
- Online Facilitator Training
- Provider's Licence
- Course Manuals
- Free Online Videos
- Prompt Online Support

METHOD

1. Select volunteers with compassion.
2. Access the Circuit Breaker app or website and join the online training school
3. Complete the Facilitator Training Course & Provider's Licence.
4. Order the Facilitator manuals.
5. Schedule a ten-week block, and launch your online programme

HELPING CHURCHES EQUIP ORDINARY PEOPLE WITH TOOLS TO PREVENT **DOMESTIC VIOLENCE** IN THEIR COMMUNITIES

LIVES TRANSFORMED

"I really feel disappointed that I didn't do this course before I came into prison because if I had, I wouldn't have had to be here. But now I can't wait to teach these skills to my sons so that they don't have to end up living the life that I did."

PRISONER SAM

FIND OUT MORE

 *nayba.org/resources/circuitbreaker*

 *@circuitbreakermovement*

 *@circuitbreakercourse*

GLOBALLY

85%

of people have

LOW SELF ESTEEM

leading to Anxiety and Depression

STEPS

> "STEPS helped me to find ways of helping myself to think differently, react differently, and more importantly, to receive God's help and forgiveness.
>
> COURSE PARTICIPANT

STEPS

THE NEED

- Anxiety disorders are the most common mental illness in the U.S. affecting 18.1% of the population. They are highly treatable, yet only 36.9% of those suffering receive treatment. [20]
- It's estimated that roughly 85% of people worldwide have low self-esteem. [20]
- Low self-esteem has been linked to violent behaviour, school dropout rates, teenage pregnancy, suicide, and low academic achievement. [20]
- Living with low self-esteem can harm mental health and lead to problems such as depression and anxiety. [20]

THE PROJECT

STEPS helps local churches support people who are struggling with unhelpful or addictive behaviours by offering a 12 week course through which people can discover new freedom.

Everybody struggles with something. From insecurity and fear to anxiety, addiction, low self-esteem and anger issues. These thoughts and patterns of behaviour stop us from living our lives to the full.

Most people think that people in churches have all the answers and that churches are waiting for people to come and ask them questions. STEPS creates an environment where those joining can participate on an equal footing, all together working on an unhelpful behaviour in their lives.

INGREDIENTS

- Two volunteer group facilitators for every 6 participants
- Video meeting platform eg Zoom or Teams
- Facilitators manual & links to STEPS films
- Participants workbook

METHOD

1. Recruit two group facilitators for every 6 anticipated participants
2. Read the STEPS Facilitators Manual
3. Invite people to an introduction session
4. Encourage participants to sign-up and purchase the course book
5. Deliver the weekly online group session

HELPING CHURCHES SUPPORT PEOPLE STRUGGLING WITH **UNHELPFUL BEHAVIOURS** TO FIND **FREEDOM**

LIVES TRANSFORMED

"I decided to do STEPS because I had heard so many great stories about how it had helped people overcome behaviour patterns they'd been struggling with. I wasn't sure what I would work on beforehand, but I decided to tackle my overriding thought patterns regarding my weight. I'd struggled with it my whole life and so it almost felt like a very 'normal' struggle', and just something I had to live with. When I look back on the journey, I can now see how far I've come, where God met me and how he kept gently revealing issues that I needed to work on, to set me free from my struggle.

ELIZABETH

FIND OUT MORE

 *nayba.org/resources/steps*

 *@thestepscourse*

@stepscourse

GLOBALLY
34% children
live in
BROKEN
FAMILY
situations

COACH
“
A series of tragic events set my life on a different path. I felt a failure. COACH embraced my whole family. Now my heart is open to new possibilities.
PARTICIPANT

COACH

THE NEED

- More than **2 out of 3 children** today are living in what would be considered a non-traditional family environment. [21]
- **34% of children** today are living with an unmarried parent. [21]
- 1 in 8 children today are born to a teen mother. [21]
- 1 in 3 children today are born to parents that are unmarried. [21]
- 1 out of every 25 kids in the United States does not live with either one of their parents. [21]

THE PROJECT

COACH helps local churches to strengthen communities by providing one-to-one mentoring tools to individuals and families, helping them to transform their lives. COACH iaims to empower individuals and families through one-to-one mentoring, breaking generational cycles of poverty and family breakdown.

Local churches are provided with a training app, which includes materials and videos to enable them to be effective mentors. All the necessary policies and procedures to ensure safety are provided, which enable the time and energy of volunteers to go towards relationship building.

COACH mobilises ordinary people for extra-ordinary community transformation.

INGREDIENTS

- Families in your community that are doing life tough
- Church volunteers with a heart for people doing life tough and able to coach (listen, question and support)
- A lead volunteer to co-ordinate the programme

METHOD

1. Contact the COACH team to discuss what is required from a local church
2. Arrange for volunteers to complete COACH training and screening
3. Recruit struggling families who need help
4. Match volunteer mentors with families
5. Provide support to volunteer mentors and monitor outcomes

HELPING CHURCHES TO MOBILISE **ORDINARY PEOPLE** FOR **EXTRA-ORDINARY** COMMUNITY **TRANSFORMATION**

LIVES TRANSFORMED

Two women from two generations and cultures have found peace, courage and new skills from a five-year mentoring relationship. Mentor Neisha said she suffered from debilitating anxiety as a child growing up in India, but unlike Chloe who has had a mentor, had to battle her fears alone. Teenager Chloe continues:

"I had anxiety and needed someone to talk to about things, Neisha's a good listener and communicates well. I've grown in confidence, particularly since coming to high school. I'm much more willing to try new things and speak up."

NEISHA & CHLOE

FIND OUT MORE

nayba.org/resources/coach

@coachcomunitymentoring

@coachcomunitymentoring

GLOBALLY

970 million

people have a

MENTAL HEALTH

disorder

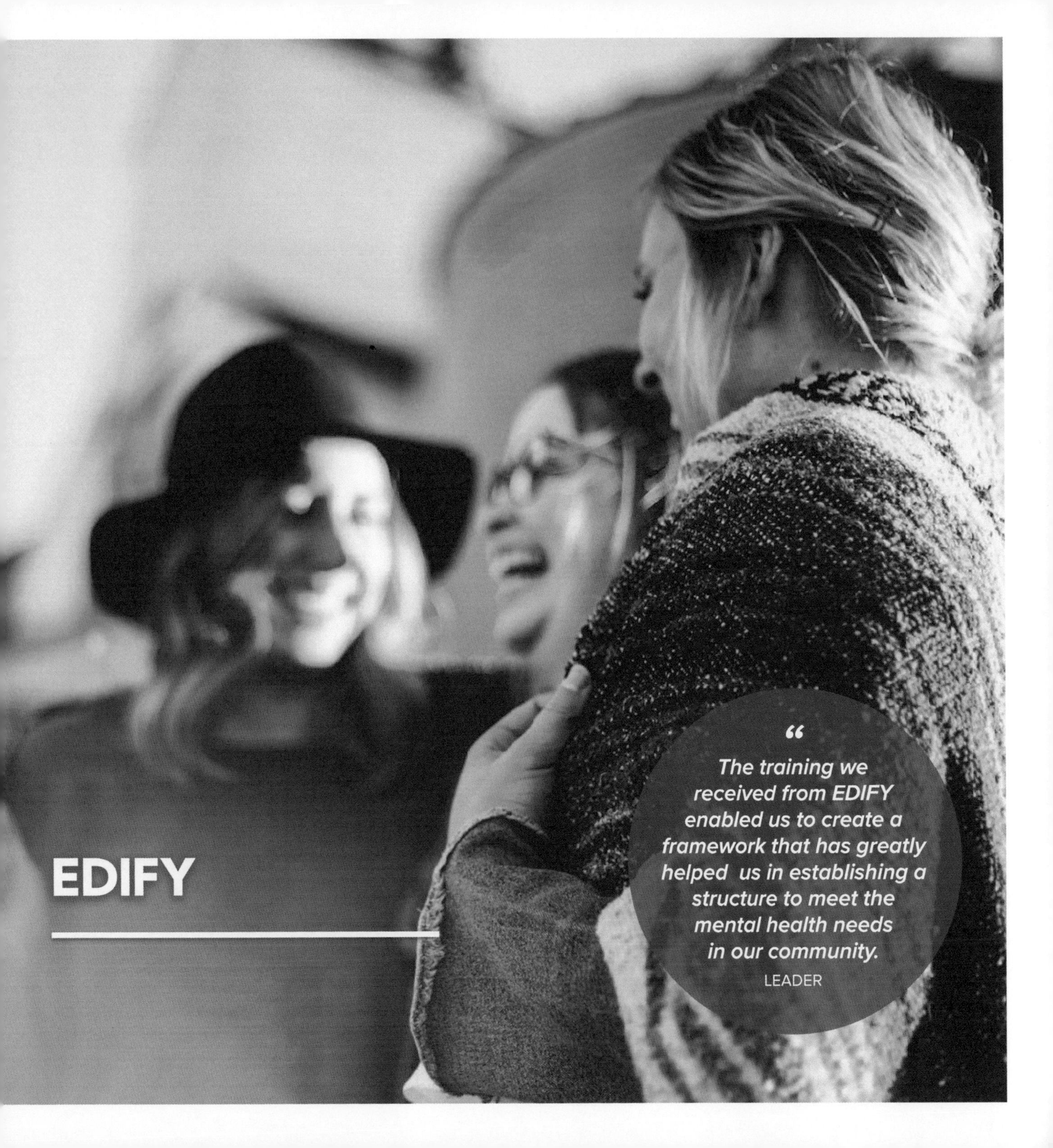
EDIFY
"
The training we received from EDIFY enabled us to create a framework that has greatly helped us in establishing a structure to meet the mental health needs in our community.
LEADER

EDIFY

THE NEED

- 970 million people worldwide had a mental health or substance abuse disorder in 2017. [22]
- Anxiety is the most common mental illness in the world, affecting 284 million people. [22]
- The mortality rate of those with mental disorders is significantly higher than the general population. It is estimated that mental disorders are attributable to approximately 8 million deaths each year. [22]
- Globally there is a growing demand for counselling therapy, which was exacerbated by the pandemic.

THE PROJECT

EDIFY helps local churches address mental health needs in their communities by equipping them with counselling training resources.

Communities turn to their local churches for support when they are in a spiritual and emotional crisis. Churches have a desire to meet their local communities needs however, they often miss connecting effectively in an emotional crisis due to a lack of counselling resources.

Resources offered by EDIFY cover Self Care, Community Care and Pastoral Care, giving churches practical tools to offer hope to communities struggling with mental health needs.

INGREDIENTS

- Pastoral Counselling Champion
- Marketing platform for resources awareness
- Mature Volunteers willing to be trained as pastoral care counsellors
- A venue for creating pastoral care counselling rooms
- Desire for maintaining a thriving pastoral care lay counselling ministry.

METHOD

1. Identity a Pastoral Counselling Champion
2. Invest in self care resources
3. Invest in community-care resources for empowerment to serve
4. Casting a net for identifying a pastoral care team willing to be trained
5. Investing in pastoral-care resources for training and establishing this care team

HELPING CHURCHES ADDRESS **MENTAL HEALTH NEEDS** IN OUR COMMUNITIES BY PROVIDING **COUNSELLING TRAINING RESOURCES**

LIVES TRANSFORMED

"Over the years we have had many lay counsellors volunteering their time to assist people, in and out of the local church community. One of the major challenges has been consistency in approach and the ability to manage progress with difficult scenarios. The training that we received from EDIFY has enabled us to put a base line, or framework, in place that has greatly assisted in establishing some structure, to manage these challenges. EDIFY provide great training for new or experienced counsellors!"

PASTOR

FIND OUT MORE

 *nayba.org/resources/edify*

 *@edifybuildingthesoul*

 *@edify_building_the_soul*

GLOBALLY

284 million

people are affected by

ANXIETY

264 million

with

DEPRESSION

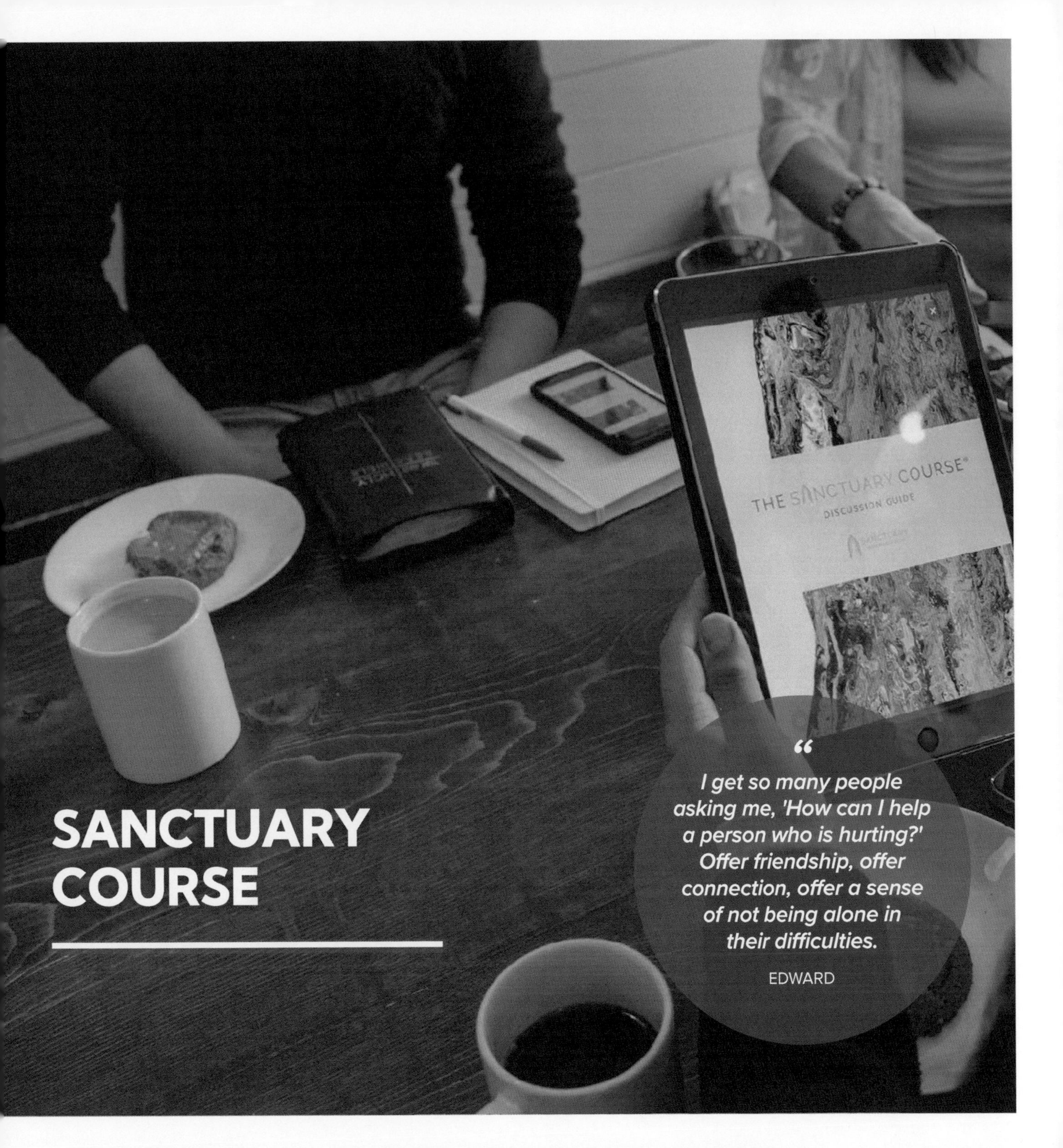

SANCTUARY COURSE

> “I get so many people asking me, 'How can I help a person who is hurting?' Offer friendship, offer connection, offer a sense of not being alone in their difficulties.
>
> EDWARD

SANCTUARY COURSE

THE NEED

- Depression affects 264 million people globally. [23]
- Anxiety affects 284 million people. [23]
- Alcohol use disorder affects 107 million people. [23]
- Drug use disorder affects 71 million people. [23]
- Bipolar disorder affects 46 million people. [23]

THE PROJECT

The Sanctuary Course was created to equip churches to become sanctuaries where individuals with mental health challenges can feel safe, supported, and gain a sense of belonging.

The course is a free eight-session resource designed for small groups which includes compelling films, a coursebook, an audiobook, and a discussion guide designed to inspire conversation and deeper reflection. Each session explores key mental health topics, drawing on the insights of mental health professionals, church leaders, and people with lived experience of mental health challenges.

These resources prepare communities of faith around the world to raise awareness, reduce stigma, and promote mental wellbeing.

INGREDIENTS

- Register on Sanctuary's online resource portal
- Access all downloadable resources needed for the course
- Participants with a desire to learn about faith and mental health with no previous training or experience needed
- Facilitators - anyone with a desire to create a safe space for conversation and learning

METHOD

1. Identity Participants and Facilitators and register them on the resource portal
2. It is recommended that each course is run in a small group of twelve or fewer. Many churches run several groups at one time.
3. Register your course online so that Sanctuary can support facilitators along the way
4. Facilitate the course at your own pace
5. Share feedback by completing the online short survey

HELPING CHURCHES TO BECOME **SANCTUARIES** WHERE PEOPLE WITH **MENTAL HEALTH** CHALLENGES FEEL **SAFE** AND **SUPPORTED**

LIVES TRANSFORMED

"As I reflect on the times in my life when I have been in a mental health crisis, I realize that most of the folks who accompanied me were not professionals, but friends who helped care for me when I could not care for myself—and who continue to support my flourishing. Accompaniment is not about fixing problems, but letting a friend know that no matter what they face, they will not face it alone. Through accompaniment, we can collaboratively find our way in landscapes that no longer feel familiar, move from languishing to flourishing, and possibly even rediscover home."

JUSTIN BARRING

FIND OUT MORE

nayba.org/resources/sanctuary

@sanctuarymentalhealth

@sanctuarymentalhealth

ENGLAND

4 million

people report living in

SOCIAL ISOLATION

now recognised as a serious

health risk

LISTENING HUBS

> “
> ***Some of the nicest friendliest people on the planet... They were friendly even having never met me before. Just the way a church should be and should do.***
>
> RUSSELL

LISTENING HUBS

THE NEED

- Social isolation is an objective lack of social contacts, which can be measured by the number of relationships a person has. Someone who is socially isolated isn't necessarily lonely, nor is a lonely person necessarily socially isolated. [24]
- There is a growing body of research that identifies and quantifies the impact of social isolation and loneliness on individuals and the wider community.
- Research by Holt-Lunstad states that 'weak social connections carry a health risk that is more harmful than not exercising, twice as harmful as obesity, and is comparable to smoking fifteen cigarettes a day or being an alcoholic.' [24]

THE PROJECT

Listening Hubs help the local church to provide a listening ear service in the heart of the community, providing a safe place for people to come and talk and be listened to by trained volunteers.

The church develops a Community Hub, providing a regular space for a range of activities such as a coffee bar, activities for children, wellbeing courses and more. Listening Hub volunteers are trained to be on hand to listen well when they're in conversation with those who need to speak out their worries and cares.

INGREDIENTS

- An attractive venue easily accessible to the community
- A range of appealing activities which will draw the local community to visit
- A team of volunteers who are inspired to provide a listening ear
- Access to suitable training material
- A range of services that people can be referred to for further help

METHOD

1. An unthreatening appealing community event or activity
2. A venue attractive to the local community
3. A team of volunteers inspired to be trained to listen well
4. A counselling training programme
5. An advertising strategy that clearly invites the community to come and chat around a range of community needs

HELPING CHURCHES TO PROVIDE A **LISTENING EAR** — A SAFE PLACE IN THE COMMUNITY FOR PEOPLE TO **TALK AND BE HEARD**

LIVES TRANSFORMED

"It's very informal, we don't sort of like put up a sign 'here's the listening hub zone'. But we make it known that you can come and if you just want to speak to someone we have people that would be more than happy to listen to you, people we trust and who are ready to listen. Our whole building is set out, like a social coffee bar, and there are plenty of places within the area to just sit and have conversation. It's very informal really and we train our volunteers to be good listeners. And the local people love it, its become a feature of our community life."

VOLUNTEER

FIND OUT MORE

 *nayba.org/resources/listeninghubs*

 *@cheritonbaptist*

 *@cheritonbaptist*

GLOBALLY
151 million
children live
WITHOUT PARENTAL CARE
and are at risk

KIDS HOPE

> *"What's happening through our Kids Hope programme excites me and our Church more than almost any other outreach or community connection we have.*
>
> MARK RIESSON
> PASTOR

KIDS HOPE

THE NEED

- Statistics show that the number of children living without parental care is rising.
- There are an estimated 151 million children worldwide who have lost one or both parents, with at least 13 million of these children having lost both parents (about 10%). [25]
- UNICEF4 estimates that there are currently 570 million children living below the poverty line of $1.25 a day. [25]

THE PROJECT

Kids Hope helps the local church adopt a local primary school and provide mentors to children experiencing vulnerability.

Volunteers give one hour a week to help children increase their resilience, confidence and well-being, bringing care and hope to children in need of extra support.

Kids Hope provide a researched and evidence-based mentoring model with proven effectiveness. Local churches are trained and resourced to deliver the mentoring, and are also assistede to facilitate partnerships with local schools.

The crucial aspect of this project is the one mentor, one child model, as a child feels special knowing that the mentor is there just for them. An hour a week for a lifetime of lasting change!

INGREDIENTS

- One volunteer coordinator
- Training materials
- Volunteer mentors
- Link to online mentoring resources
- One child, One mentor, One hour a week (during school term)

METHOD

1. Assign a volunteer coordinator
2. Coordinator is trained to recruit, screen and train mentors
3. Coordinator leads in-church recruitment of mentors using resources, supplied
4. Coordinator meets with school principal to share the model
5. School selects students and matches are made with volunteer mentors

HELPING CHURCHES WORK WITH LOCAL PRIMARY SCHOOLS TO PROVIDE **MENTORS TO CHILDREN** EXPERIENCING VULNERABILITY

LIVES TRANSFORMED

"The look in their eye gives it away
How special must I be that you've come today!
So what shall we do?
And what shall we say?
I'm really just happy that you're here today.

But sometimes I feel so sad inside,
So little and so small, I don't feel very special,
Not a little not at all.
But to know that you are coming,
And will not delay, I know in my heart
I must be special in some way."

poem sent by A CHILD

FIND OUT MORE

 *nayba.org/resources/kidshope*

 *@KidsHopeAustralia*

 *@KidsHopeAustralia*

ENTERPRISE

GLOBALLY

220 million

people were logged as

UNEMPLOYED

an increase of

33 million

due to the pandemic

THE SPIRIT OF ENTERPRISE

> *"I'm delighted that we were the first church to run the Enterprise Course. I thought it was a fantastic opportunity for our church to reach out into the community.*
>
> NEAL STANTON

THE SPIRIT OF ENTERPRISE

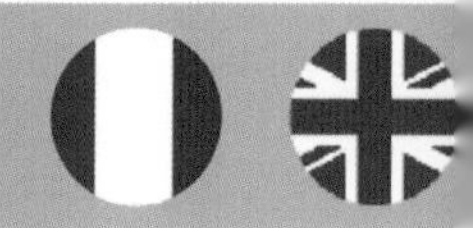

THE NEED

- Soaring food and energy prices have resulted in 71 million people in developing countries falling into poverty. [26]
- In the UK, as many as 1 in 7 adults now say they can't afford to eat every day — an increase of 57% since January 2022. [26]
- One job is not enough for 5.2 million UK workers as the cost of living crisis continues to bite, with a further 10 million workers considering taking on another job if costs continue to rise. [26]

THE PROJECT

The Spirit of Enterprise enables churches to help people facing financial hardship to start a business as a lasting solution to poverty.

The Spirit of Enterprise course is a seven session course that helps people come up with an idea for a business and then plan its launch. The course can be delivered once a week for seven weeks, or alternate weeks for 14 weeks, or whatever frequency suits.

A Spirit of Enterprise hub is an ecosystem of support a church provides people who graduate from the course and start a business. The church provides shared office space where entrepreneurs can support each other and an enterprise mentor can guide and support them to get their enterprise started and growing.

INGREDIENTS

- A lead volunteer who is a business person
- A venue to host a relaxed connect event.
- A venue to host a seven session course.
- A venue to host a shared office space.
- The Spirit of Enterprise book from Amazon.
- The Spirit of Enterprise leaders guide free from NAYBA

METHOD

1. Register with NAYBA to receive the Spirit of Enterprise free leaders guide and support
2. Host a Spirit of Enterprise Connect event to introduce the course to potential participants
3. Facilitate the seven-session Spirit of Enterprise course to enable participants to conceive and launch an enterprise
4. Launch a Spirit of Enterprise Hub as a support base for people launching a new business.
5. Repeat!

HELPING CHURCHES ENABLE PEOPLE WHO ARE FACING FINANCIAL HARDSHIP TO START A BUSINESS

LIVES TRANSFORMED

"The Spirit of Enterprise Course showed me how my art can be an enterprise. I have set up a business concentrating on the three different areas I work in: photography, design and printing. The course enabled me to take that leap of faith and create a business. It has given me the confidence to grow and to communicate with people better. I was not expecting to come out of the other side with a fully running idea for a business. It's not something I ever imagined."

ANDRÉ VAN-THOMAS

FIND OUT MORE

 *nayba.org/resources/thespiritofenterprisecourse*

 *@naybaglobal*

 *@naybaglobal*

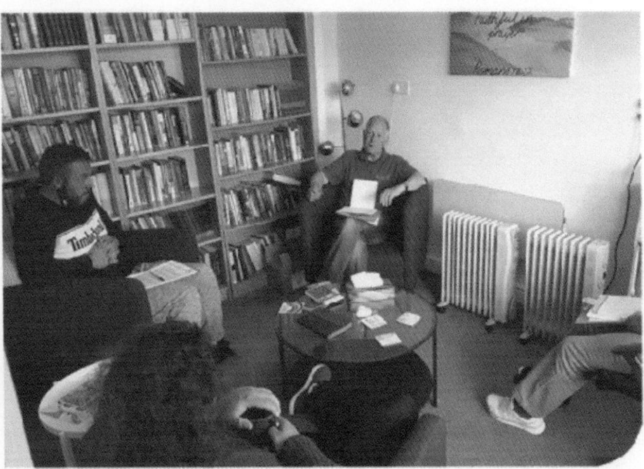

ALBANIA

34%

people live in

POVERTY

5.8%

in extreme poverty

SMALL TRACTORS

> "We realised that if we wanted to help bring change in the community, it would only come when people can work and improve their lives by working, not by waiting for others to help.
>
> ALMA SYLA

SMALL TRACTORS

THE NEED

- In 2016, 34% of Albanians lived in poverty, and 5.8% in extreme poverty surviving on less than $1.90/day. [27]
- The unemployment rate in Albania stood at 11.47% in 2019, before the pandemic; [27]
- The poorest in Albania tend to live in the most rural of regions. Farming is one of the primary sources of income for this group of people. Many have to make ends meet by farming in mountains where small amounts of crops can get yielded from the soil.

THE PROJECT

The **Small Tractor** project helps local churches in Albania to provide practical farming assistance to poor families in rural villages, enabling them to work the land and provide income.

A few years ago a church in Lushnjë in Albania initiated the Small Tractor Project. Their idea was to make small tractors available to very poor families in a nearby village to enable them to work the land and to provide income for their families.

This project has helped the local church show God's love and care for poor families in a very practical way. It has transformed lives in the community by providing more income for feeding their families and improving their general well-being.

INGREDIENTS

- A project leader with a heart for helping people and some knowledge of farming
- Access to an impoverished rural community
- A community of families who have the willingness to farm the land
- Through research identify the unique needs of the community and the tools needed
- A plan to raise funds to purchase the relevant agricultural equipment for the region

METHOD

1. Research the rural area to determine if farming is viable in the community
2. Build relationship with families in the area
3. Embark on a fund-raising drive to raise funds to purchase the necessary equipment
4. Arrange an event to handover the tractors or equipment, with training included
5. The project leader walks a constant journey with the recipients to provide the necessary support, in terms of training and know how

HELPING CHURCHES IN ALBANIA TO PROVIDE PRACTICAL **FARMING ASSISTANCE** TO **POOR FAMILIES** IN RURAL VILLAGES

LIVES TRANSFORMED

"Early on we saw that the people in the area are very poor and so we as a church started by providing groceries for them. This was a good way of solving an immediate problem but we wanted them to be able to have the dignity of providing for themselves. So we came up with an idea to provide small tractors to enable them to work their own land. Since then we have seen that these families not only work for themselves, but are also helping other families by letting them make use of the tractors as well. In this way they are not only providing for themselves but have grown a good relationship with their neighbours."

VOLUNTEER

FIND OUT MORE

nayba.org/resources/smalltractors

@NAYBAAlbania

@NAYBAAlbania

GLOBALLY

698 million

people live in

EXTREME POVERTY

living on less than

$1.90/day

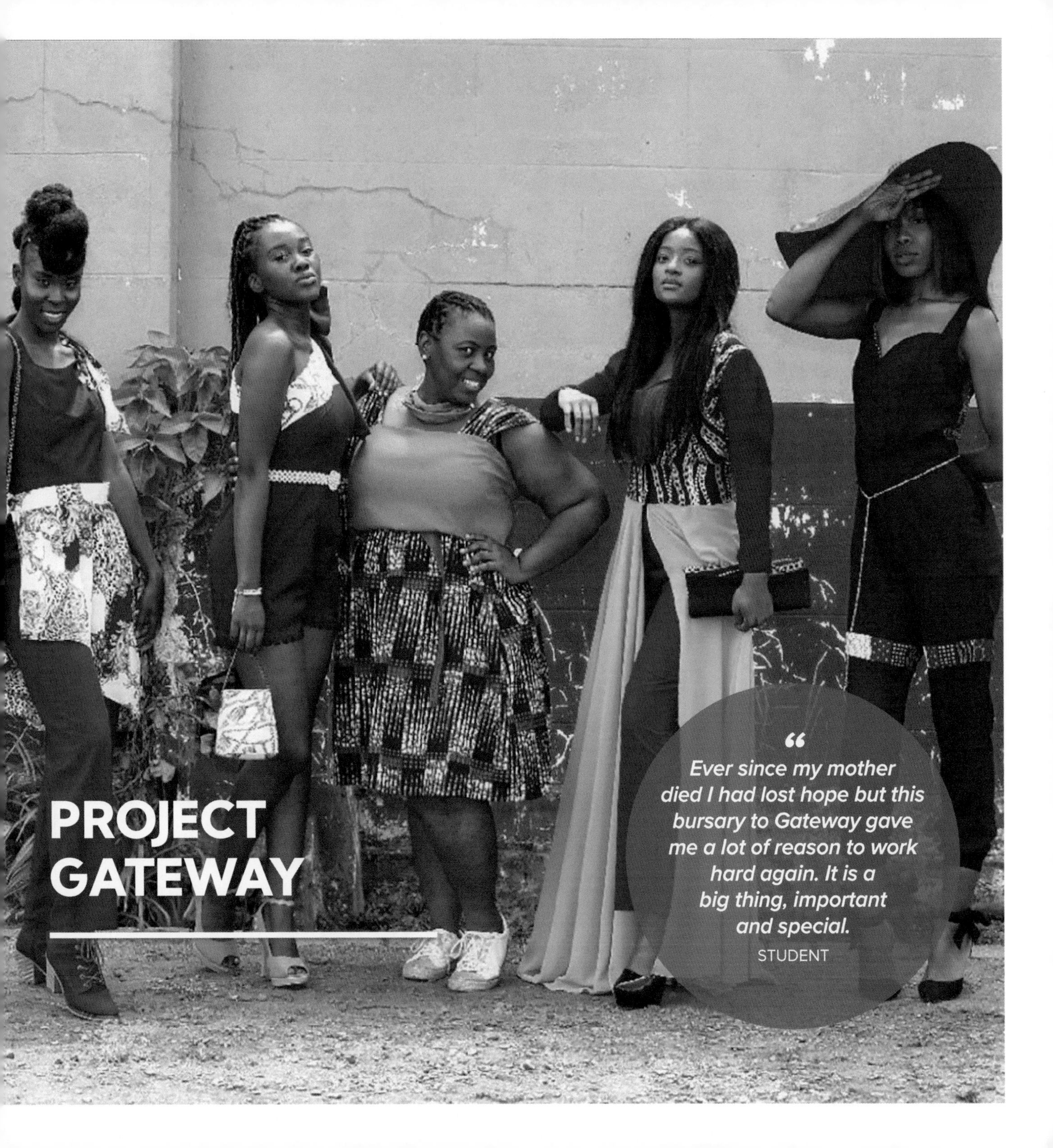
PROJECT
GATEWAY
"
Ever since my mother
died I had lost hope but this
bursary to Gateway gave
me a lot of reason to work
hard again. It is a
big thing, important
and special.
STUDENT

PROJECT GATEWAY

THE NEED

- In 2021 an estimated 698 million people, or 9% of the global population, are living in extreme poverty – that is, living on less than $1.90 a day. [28]
- Given South Africa's alarming statistics around poverty, unemployment, HIV/AIDS pandemic levels, and the vulnerability of certain groups within the society, Gateway's aim is to run effective and dynamic programmes, changing lives and impacting communities.

THE PROJECT

Project Gateway helps churches to assist people trapped in poverty by providing Care, Education and Empowerment.

The first priority when finding communities in crisis is to care for people's immediate needs such as food, shelter and clothing. Once these needs are addressed churches are equipped to help people rise out of the poverty trap by providing enterprise programmes which educate and empower them.

- the Care Programme supports local crèches, after school care centres and community gardens;
- the Education Programme has set up a primary school model providing quality education;
- the Empowerment Programmes comprises a Business Training Course, a School of Fashion, Computer Literacy Classes and a Mentorship Programme for local crafters

INGREDIENTS

- A community in crisis
- A lead volunteer with a passion to serve the vulnerable
- Volunteer helpers who can be trained
- An equipped and suitable venue within the community
- The ability to gather the necessary resources including food, shelter and educational equipment

METHOD

1. Contact the Gateway Project and receive training tools
2. Recruit a lead volunteer and team
3. Decide which of the three empowerment programmes to focus on
4. Facilitate training of all helpers
5. Secure a suitable venue in the local area
6. Plan and execute the programme

HELPING CHURCHES SUPPORT PEOPLE **TRAPPED IN POVERTY** BY PROVIDING **CARE, EDUCATION** AND **EMPOWERMENT**

LIVES TRANSFORMED

"I would firstly like to thank you for the bursary to Gateway school. It is a big thing, important and special. Ever since my mother died I had lost hope but this bursary gave me a lot of reason to work hard again. I have no special words that can tell you how much I appreciate this but my actions can - I am work hard with pride and dedication. What you did for me is a very kind thing. May God bless you."

letter from a CHILD

FIND OUT MORE

 *nayba.org/resources/projectgateway*

 *@ProjectGatewayKZN*

 *@projectgateway30*

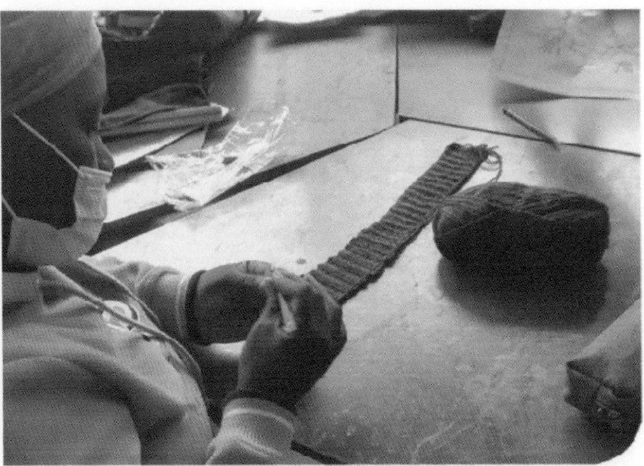

UNITED KINGDOM

4.29 million

workers are

SELF EMPLOYED

with

5.5 million

small businesses

MIND YOUR OWN BUSINESS

> “
> ***I love being self employed and running my own business and the freedom that comes from that. And also the ability for me as a Christian to bless the community.***
> ENTREPRENEUR

MIND YOUR OWN BUSINESS

THE NEED

- Following Brexit, two general elections, and a global pandemic, the past five years have been a particularly difficult time for small business owners. [29]
- This triple disruption has played a big role in the rising cost of living, and the decline of the number of small businesses in the UK to 5.5 million. [29]
- However, SMEs account for 99.9% of the UK's business population. This total is a clear indication of the important role small businesses continue to play in the national economy. [29]

THE PROJECT

The **Mind Your Own Business** programme helps churches to reach out to those in their local community who may be unemployed and are interested in starting their own business. It offers practical material that can be helpful to anyone starting a business whether they are believers or not.

The Course is something that can be done around a kitchen table with three or four people working through the material themselves, or it can be done in a church building with a group of 20 or so people run by a facilitator and mentors. It's highly relevant in our post-covid world as, typically, more people are wanting to become self employed, and therefore this model is very timely.

INGREDIENTS

- A facilitator with some business knowledge who is inspired to help other entrepreneurs
- The Mind Your Own Business course material downloaded from the website
- A suitable venue that is available for the duration of the course
- Participants keen to run their own business
- An agreed programme communicated — start date, number and duration of sessions

METHOD

1. Identify someone in the church who has experience of running a business or is entrepreneurial in nature
2. Visit the MYOB website and become acquainted with the course material
3. Promote the concept in the local community
4. Recruit people who are wanting to start their own business
5. Find a suitable venue and set up a start date and course programme

HELPING CHURCHES REACH THOSE IN THEIR COMMUNITY WHO ARE **UNEMPLOYED** AND WOULD LIKE TO START **THEIR OWN BUSINESS**

LIVES TRANSFORMED

"I just wanted you to know I have just completed your wonderful "Mind Your Own Business" course and must say it is so comprehensive I'm immensely impressed and this is coming from an experienced Transition Life Coach. For anyone reading this, if you're looking for a road map about starting a business, take a look at this free resource. You will benefit greatly by taking advantage of this important programme."

COURSE PARTICIPANT

FIND OUT MORE

 *nayba.org/resources/mindyourownbusiness*

 *https://mindyourownbusiness.uk*

SOUTH AFRICA

7.9 million

young people are

JOBLESS

which equates to a

34%

unemployment rate

PARADIGM SHIFT

> *"It was God who placed the dream in my heart to see entrepreneurs in poor communities break free from poverty. I was just a Christian businesswoman with a burning dream in my heart.*
>
> VOLUNTEER

PARADIGM SHIFT

THE NEED

- In South Africa in 2022 the total employment increased by 370 000 to 14,9 million compared to the previous quarter, while unemployment declined by 60 000 to 7,9 million, resulting in the official unemployment rate of 34,5%. [30]
- South Africa has over 10 million young people aged 15-24 years and, of these, only 2,5 million are active in the labour force. 7,7 million young people are those that are inactive and out of the labour force. The main reason for being inactive is discouragement. [30]

THE PROJECT

Paradigm Shift helps the local church to transform the lives of those who have chosen entrepreneurship as a way out of poverty, by equipping micro-entrepreneurs with business training, mentoring and discipleship.

The church identifies a Point Person, who is trained to recruit and train a group of 5 other volunteer trainers. With a target community in mind, they run an introductory One-Day Business Experience Course (one or more times), before selecting the best micro-entrepreneurs to proceed through a 9-week journey of business training and discipleship.

INGREDIENTS

- A team of six volunteers with business experience
- A free Saturday
- A training venue
- A desire to coach entrepreneurs in small business skills
- An ability to prayerfully disciple others in faith
- A Paradigm Shift Training Kit

METHOD

1. Identity a Point Person (Lead Volunteer)
2. Recruit a Volunteer Team of 6 people
3. Train the Volunteer Team
4. Invite Micro-Entrepreneurs from the community
5. Train Micro-Entrepreneurs

HELPING CHURCHES TRANSFORM THE LIVES OF THOSE WHO HAVE CHOSEN **ENTREPRENEURSHIP** AS A WAY OUT OF **POVERTY**

LIVES TRANSFORMED

“I stood beside her hospital bed, scarcely recognizing the emaciated woman lying against the white sheets. She was a shadow of the woman I’d met just one year earlier. We came from two different worlds, though we were only a few miles apart.

Nokusa lived in a tin-roofed shack in a community where rats raced across the dirt roads. I lived in a neighborhood of homes with crowded pantries and flat-screen TVs. I was the first “white friend” she ever had. Nokusa’s strength and faith have left a mark on my life. I was Nokusa’s mentor, but she taught me much more than I taught her”

GLENIS

FIND OUT MORE

 *nayba.co/resources/paradigmshift*

 *@ParadigmShiftsa*

 *@projectgateway30*

THE NEED

1. DEMENTIA
   WHO - World Health Organisation : 'Dementia' https://www.who.int/news-room/fact-sheets/detail/dementia

2. POST PARTUM DEPRESSION
   NIH - National Library of Medicine : Prevalence of postpartum depression and interventions ...
   https://www.ncbi.nlm.nih.gov/pmc/articles/PMC5941764/
   Mainly Ministries research https://mainlyministries.org/

3. YOUTH & LANGUAGE IN ALBANIA
   USAID - Fact Sheet: Support for Albanian Youth
   https://www.usaid.gov/albania/news-information/fact-sheets/fact-sheet-youth

4. LONELINESS
   Campaign To End Lonelienss https://www.campaigntoendloneliness.org/the-facts-on-loneliness/

5. HOMELESSNESS IN AUSTRALIA
   Australian Institute of Health & Welfare : Homelessness
   https://www.aihw.gov.au/reports/australias-welfare/homelessness-and-homelessness-services

6. CHILDREN IN THEIR FIRST 1000 DAYS OF LIFE
   Christian Journal for Global Health : The Local Church and the First Thousand Days of a Child's Life: A Mixed Methods Study from South Africa https://journal.cjgh.org/index.php/cjgh/article/view/323
   SIKUNYE - We Are Together - Research https://sikunye.org.za/the-big-idea/research/

7. COFFEE CULTURE ALBANIA
   Breathe In Travel - A guide to Albania's coffee culture
   https://breatheintravel.com/2022/04/05/albania-coffee-culture-guide/
   Experience Cafe Culture https://inlovewithalbania.com/cafes-in-albania/

8. CRIME IN SOUTH AFRICA
   Christian World Population in Review : Crime rate by country
   https://worldpopulationreview.com/country-rankings/crime-rate-by-country
   PSA Report 2017 : The state and safety of police officers in the line of duty
   https://www.psa.co.za/docs/default-source/psa-documents/psa-opinion/psa_police_2017.pdf?sfvrsn=21e36d8c_3

9. PRISONERS AUSTRALIA
   United Nations Office on Drugs & Crime Report 2021
   https://www.unodc.org/documents/data-and-analysis/statistics/DataMatters1_prison.pdf
   Australian Bureau of Statistics 2021

IMPACT DATA SOURCES

10. FATHERLESSNESS
    Stellenbosch Theological Journal : 'Responding to the challenge of father absence and fatherlessness in the South African context: A case study.
    http://www.scielo.org.za/pdf/stj/v3n1/07.pdf
    Stas SA Report : Damilies and parents are key to well-being of children
    https://www.statssa.gov.za/?p=14388

11. DISPLACED PEOPLE / TEMPORARY SHELTER
    European Commission : Shelter and Settlements, A factsheet.
    https://civil-protection-humanitarian-aid.ec.europa.eu/what/humanitarian-aid/shelter-and-settlements_en

12. FOOD INSECURITY AUSTRALIA
    McCrindle Research : Food insecurity in Australia
    https://mccrindle.com.au/article/food-insecurity-in-australia/

13. HOMELESSNESS
    Habitat for Humanity : World Habitat Day article
    https://www.habitat.org/volunteer/build-events/world-habitat-day

14. POVERTY GUERNSEY, CHANNNEL ISLANDS
    States of Guernsey - Advisory & Finance Committee Report : Adult and Child Poverty in Guernsey.
    http://www.bris.ac.uk/poverty/downloads/regionalpovertystudies/02_GLS-2.pdf

15. POVERTY & INJUSTICE
    Oxfam : A Tale of Two Continents - Fighting inequality in Africa
    https://www-cdn.oxfam.org/s3fs-public/file_attachments/bp-tale-of-two-continents-fighting-inequality-africa-030919-en.pdf

16. BELOW THE POVERTY LINE AUSTRALIA
    NSW Council of Social Service (NCOSS) / IZA World of Labour Report 2019
    https://wol.iza.org/news/almost-900000-people-living-in-poverty-in-nsw.

17. BROKEN WOMEN
    Mind UK - Mental Health facts and statistics
    https://www.mind.org.uk/information-support/types-of-mental-health-problems/statistics-and-facts-about-mental-health/how-common-are-mental-health-problems/
    Mental Health Foundation : Women and mental health
    https://www.mentalhealth.org.uk/explore-mental-health/a-z-topics/women-and-mental-health

THE NEED

18. ADDICTION
Our World in Data, Oxford University - article 2018, revised 2021 : Global Alcohol Consumption
https://ourworldindata.org/alcohol-consumption
Journal of Behavioural Addictions - 2020 Report
https://akjournals.com/view/journals/2006/2006-overview.xml

19. DOMESTIC VIOLENCE
WHO - World Health Organisation 2021 Global Fact Sheet : Violence against Women
https:// www.who.int/news-room/fact-sheets/detail/violence-against-women.

20. LOW SELF ESTEEM
Psychology Today : The Relationship With Yourself - notes on self-confidence and authenticity
https://www.psychologytoday.com/intl/blog/sustainable-life-satisfaction/201906/the-relationship-yourself
Life Skills South Florida: article Anxiety Disorders in the USA
https://www.lifeskillssouthflorida.com/mental-health-blog/anxiety-disorders-affecting-americans-by-the-millions/

21. FAMILY BREAKDOWN
Brandon Gaille 2017 Article: Scary Statistics on Dysfunctional Families
https://brandongaille.com/22-scarey-statistics-on-dysfunctional-families/

22. MENTAL HEALTH COUNSELLING
Our World in Data - Global Mental Health article, 2018; updated 2021
https://ourworldindata.org/mental-health
American Psychological Association article : Demand for mental health treatment increases post COVID.
https://www.apa.org/news/press/releases/2021/10/mental-health-treatment-demand

23. ANXIETY & DEPRESSION
Single Care Article : Mental health statistics 2022
https://www.singlecare.com/blog/news/mental-health-statistics/

24. SOCIAL ISOLATION IN UK
IoTUK Article : Social isolation and loneliness in the UK
https://iotuk.org.uk/wp-content/uploads/2017/04/Social-Isolation-and-Loneliness-Landscape-UK.pdf

25. VULNERABLE CHILDREN
SOS Children's Villages International : Child At Risk Report - The world's most vulnerable children
https://www.sos-childrensvillages.org/getmedia/384bc38a-62aa-4c2a-9563-a5ecc61b6a77/SOS-Child-at-risk-report-web.pdf

IMPACT DATA SOURCES

26. GLOBAL ECONOMIC CRISIS
https://www.weforum.org/agenda/2022/09/cost-of-living-crisis-global-impact/
https://www.theguardian.com/society/2022/may/09/more-than-2m-adults-in-uk-cannot-afford-to-eat-every-day-survey-finds.
https://www.royallondon.com/about-us/media/media-centre/press-releases/press-releases-2022/september/cost-of-living-crisis-leaves-millions-taking-on-second-job/

27. UNEMPLOYMENT IN ALBANIA
World Bank - Migration and Mobilty Report : Albanians live on poverty
https://exit.al/en/2017/10/25/world-bank-34-of-albanians-live-in-poverty/

28. POVERTY & NEED FOR SKILLS DEVELOPMENT
Development Initiatives Factsheet 2021 : Poverty trends - global, regional and national
https://devinit.org/resources/poverty-trends-global-regional-and-national/

29. SELF EMPLOYMENT IN THE UK
Statista 2022 : Number of self-employed workers in the UK 1992-2022
https://www.statista.com/statistics/318234/united-kingdom-self-employed/
Startups Article : Small Business Statistics 2022
https://startups.co.uk/analysis/small-business-statistics/

30. UNEMPLOYMENT IN SOUTH AFRICA
Stats SA 2022 Quarterly Labour Force Survey
https://www.statssa.gov.za/publications/P0211/Presentation%20QLFS%20Q1%202022.pdf
Stats SA Article : South Africa's youth continues to bear the burden of unemployment.
https://www.statssa.gov.za/?p=15407

ABOUT **NAYBA**

NAYBA is a global foundation that helps churches love their neighbours and transform their neighbourhoods.

- **NAYBA Replicate** supports churches to discern community needs and opportunities and choose from a menu of tried-and-tested church-led community projects that have a track-recond for social impact.
- **NAYBA Civic** enables churches in a local government area to work together to lead an 'Impact Audit' to measure their collective social and economic impact in order to catalyse their civic transformation journey.
- **NAYBA Enterprise** resources churches to run 'The Spirit of Enterprise' course and hubs to help people facing financial hardship to start a business as a lasting solution to poverty.

NAYBA is supporting churches in more than twenty countries across four continents and welcomes your partnership.

www.NAYBA.org

OTHER **NAYBA** BOOKS

TRANSFORM
Helping churches transform neighbourhoods

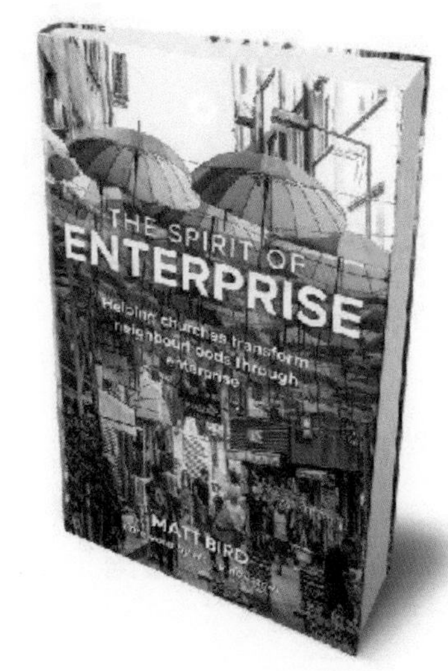

THE SPIRIT OF
ENTERPRISE
Helping churches transform neighbourhoods through enterprise

CIVIC
Helping churches transform neighbourhoods through public square engagement

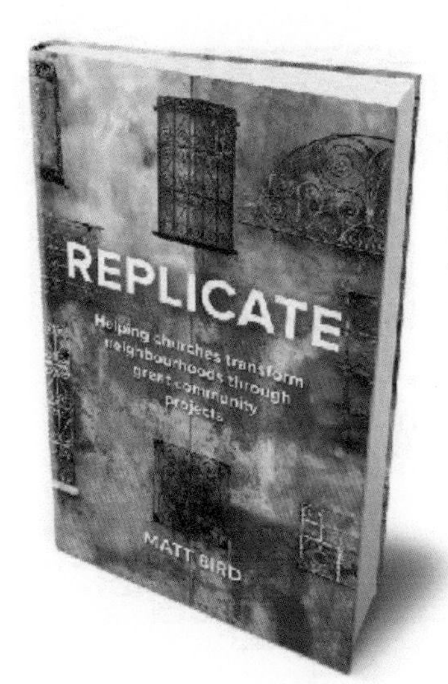

REPLICATE
Helping churches transform neighbourhoods through great community projects

Printed in Great Britain
by Amazon